Super Simple Birdhouses You Can Make

Super Simple Birdhouses You Can Make

Charles R. Self

Sterling Publishing Co., Inc.   New York

Acknowledgments

Much credit goes to other people for this book, with special thanks to my wife, Frances, for helping me arrange my schedule so the work was done at least close to schedule. Jim Ray of McFeely's provided some sample square-drive screws for tests—tests that proved to me there's truly a substantive difference in ease of use between these and other screws. Woodcraft and The Woodworker's Store provided some very important assistance, as did the following companies: Trend-Lines, California Redwood Association, Cherry Tree Toys, Freud, Stanley Tools, Cooper Tools (Plumb, Lufkin), Porter-Cable, Delta, Dremel, Makita, DeWalt, Black & Decker, Skil (now S-B Power Tools), Parks Corporation, UGL, Irwin (now part of American Tool Companies), Franklin International, Stanley Hardware, Vermont-American, Sears, Roebuck & Co., Ryobi of America. Finally, thanks to Paul Meisel, of Meisel Hardware, who provided doors, windows, and encouragement for this and other books . . . and my apologies to anyone I forgot to thank along the way.

* * *

Library of Congress Cataloging-in-Publication Data

Self, Charles R.
    Super simple birdhouses you can make / Charles Self.
        p.   cm.
    Includes index.
    ISBN 0-8069-0858-0
    1. Birdhouses—Design and construction. I. Title.
QL676.5.S385 1995
690′.89—dc20   95-20392
                                    CIP

3 5 7 9 10 8 6 4 2

Published by Sterling Publishing Company, Inc.
387 Park Avenue South, New York, N.Y. 10016
© 1995 by Charles Self
Distributed in Canada by Sterling Publishing
℅ Canadian Manda Group, One Atlantic Avenue, Suite 105
Toronto, Ontario, Canada M6K 3E7
Distributed in Great Britain and Europe by Cassell PLC
Wellington House, 125 Strand, London WC2R 0BB, England
Distributed in Australia by Capricorn Link (Australia) Pty Ltd.
P.O. Box 6651, Baulkham Hills, Business Centre, NSW 2153, Australia
Printed and bound in Hong Kong
All rights reserved

Sterling ISBN 0-8069-0858-0

Contents

Introduction

This is a book I've looked forward to doing for some time. When writing *Making Birdhouses & Feeders* (Sterling Publishing Co., 1985), I learned quite a bit about birdhouses. With the publication of my next book, *Making Fancy Birdhouses & Feeders* (Sterling, 1988), I had learned even more. Using this storehouse of information, I am now able to present a variety of intriguing, easy-to-make birdhouse projects. These projects range from a simple gourd to a Western-hotel birdhouse with a false front and a collapsing sign, to a birdhouse with a steeple that points its white spire towards the heavens. Cedar and redwood are the woods most often used, but other woods are employed with frequency, including some exotics such as purpleheart and zebrawood. All these designs are new, and my drawing skills are better than they were a decade ago.

Included in the following pages are birdhouse designs for many varieties of bird, including flycatchers, nuthatches, several types of wren, chickadees, robins and other thrushes, and both eastern and western bluebirds. All the birdhouse designs are simple, even those for the birdhouses that look more complicated (Illus. I–1). My overall desire was to make most of the designs easy to produce at almost any level of woodworking skill.

I've noticed a lot of birdhouse plans recently that call for copper, aluminum, and other metals for roofing materials. Part of the problem with any birdhouse design is creating one that holds some heat during cooler weeks early in the breeding season—remember, these are nesting boxes, not year-round homes—and loses excess heat during warmer days in late spring. In Virginia, where I live, we have problems with baby birds freezing to death, something that I feel is encouraged by heat-losing metal roofs. Thus, no matter what else you do to a birdhouse, use a wooden roof. If you decide to change one of my designs to use a metal roof, by all means feel free, but please place the metal over the wood or use the birdhouse for decoration only.

You'll find a number of patterns that should work quite well for craft fairs (the easy-to-clean wren house is one example). Many of the simpler designs can also be produced in quantity fairly easily (Illus. I–2), so your profits may be good (although I have trouble figuring out why anyone would *pay* for a birdhouse when they're so easy to build). Fancier designs that are also easy to make include the concave-roof wren house, which can be produced very rapidly with pneumatic tools and glue, using redwood for the house and cedar slats (instead of the strips I peeled off the top edges of cedar clapboard) for roofing. It's possible to make a roofing jig that does a neater, faster job than just the eyeballing and stapling I did on my model; almost any siding mechanic can show you what he uses, and you just need to miniaturize that.

Making birdhouses provides a lot of satisfaction that starts with the design and building of the projects and continues as you see your projects help some feathered

Illus. I–1. This martin house has an adobe motif and is the largest birdhouse in this book; nevertheless, it is easy to build.

Illus. I–2. Redwood birdhouses are placed around my yard, and have added considerably to our local bluebird population.

species cope with modern encroachments. Certainly the bluebird could never had made such a spectacular comeback without help from humans. Such help is needed, and adds to the fun of building these projects.

I hope you enjoy producing these designs as much as I did making them.

Charles R. Self

*   *   *

1. Birdhouse Construction Guidelines

This book has more than 30 simple birdhouse plans for a variety of birds, and contains a chart that lists the dimensions needed to house a specific type of bird in case you want to convert the design to attract your favorite. In many cases, when converting the design, all you need do is reduce or enlarge the size of the entry hole. For most of the plans, you need wood no longer than 12 inches and no wider than 7 inches, and you can use scrap pieces. Where wider pieces are needed, glue-up is a simple matter. The chance to reduce your scrap pile, produce useful homes for breeding birds, and enjoy woodworking and bird-watching all add to the overall enjoyment of such projects.

Two species of wood—cedar and redwood—serve perfectly well for all birdhouse construction purposes. Both are attractive woods that weather well and are very durable. Some of the bluebird house photos that appear in this book are of houses I made over four years ago, and all but one are made of clear redwood. That one is made of cedar, with a pressure-treated and painted roof.

Read Chapter Two, about construction material, carefully because there are many different types of material that can be used, even from a scrap pile, and more are possible if you're producing decorative birdhouses for sale or as gifts.

Some of the projects are done partially in purpleheart, and a number in oak. Some have a piece or two of unusual wood; for example, the roof of one birdhouse is made of paulownia and parts of another are made of sassafras. Others, such as the cabin of "logs," are made of several different woods.

You'll see a similar look on many of the roofs. I used some cedar clapboard trimmed in one manner or another to make roofs for many of the houses (Illus. 1–1.) It works nicely, and is cheap in broken lots (it cost about 25¢ a running foot a few years ago, and not much more now, if part of the length is damaged). However, other roof treatments are possible.

Much of the plywood I used is interior hardwood plywood, not meant to withstand the rigors of weather, which means the resulting birdhouse must be protected with clear finish or paint. The only acceptable clear finishes are exterior versions: Interior clear finishes lack the ultraviolet inhibitors needed to keep the finish from breaking down. Otherwise, I used Carver-Tripp enamel finishes because they're nontoxic, water-based polyurethanes that go on easily and cover well with water clean-up. For clear finishes, I used Exterior ZAR polyurethane, from UGL. Exterior ZAR requires mineral spirit clean-up, but most water-based clear polyurethanes are harder to brush on or wipe off and so weren't used.

If your birdhouses are correctly sized and placed in areas the desired species frequents, and if general plantings are such as to attract birds, then sooner or later your guests will arrive. Check the chart on pages 124 and 125 for height requirements for different species, and please remember that some species, such as cardinals and blue-jays, don't care for human-built nesting. However, many species do, and most are highly desirable birds.

* * *

Illus. 1–1. Cedar clapboard makes a fine roof material.

2. Wood Materials for Birdhouses

Wood is the favored material for constructing birdhouses. It can be easily shaped or bent with tools, wears well under abrasion, and withstands all sorts of stress. It also insulates, keeping birds cool in summer, but providing some warmth in earlier stages of the year. Many woods last well under conditions that ruin many steels and plastics. Wood is relatively cheap and naturally attractive.

While most birdhouses are constructed for use out of doors, they are now frequently being used as decorative items, often indoors, which means that the array of different woods that can be used on them is as great as for any other type of project. Many outdoor birdhouses are now getting bold coats of paint, something birds don't care for but people do.

When searching for birdhouse material, also consider using any wood you might find. I recently participated in a local Marine Corps League wood-cutting session (to help those who need fuel assistance beyond what the government supplies), and was able to place dibs on two large pieces of cedar log, enough, if I'm careful, for four turned birdhouses. And I've recently turned over my pile of wood looking for wood that's not good enough to use for fine projects but good enough for birdhouses.

A number of smaller birdhouses in this book are made completely or partially of walnut, and even more are made of red or white oak. I've even used some bits of zebrawood, purpleheart, paulownia, and one or two more exotic woods, and was tempted to use teak for one—absolutely an ideal wood, but too costly—until I realized that I had enough teak to build a small box instead. Such fancy woods may be painted, but it's a waste of paint. Coat them with an exterior clear polyurethane over wood stain for best results.

Most kinds of solid wood work well for birdhouses because boards wider than 6 or 8 inches and as long as 12 inches are seldom needed. Plywood is generally used on larger projects with wide, flat parts, so it's a good material to use on some birdhouses. Even standard construction lumber is useful for a few projects, or parts of projects.

MILLING

Commonly, trees are milled by sawing around or through the log. Both ways produce flat-grain boards, but sawing directly through the log as it is fed into the saw, with no changes in its position, produces a mix of grain figures.

Flat-sawn lumber is not the best type of lumber for precise woodworking because it is a mixture of sapwood and heartwood and its boards have edge-grain edges. It is generally suitable for birdhouse construction, unless you need really wide boards. The different densities and drying characteristics of the sapwood and heartwood mean the board will warp and cup. The wider the board, the worse the cupping. Look for U- or V-shaped markings at the ends of the boards. If you see those shapes, then the lumber is flat-sawn.

Quartersawn lumber is cut at a 90-degree angle to the growth rings. There is less of a mix of heartwood and sapwood in each board, so the board has less tendency to warp and cup. Quartersawn lumber costs more than flat-sawn lumber, warps less, and is more easily worked, but is generally too good for use as a birdhouse material.

Wood forms vary considerably, and some are better suited to birdhouse construction than are others, though virtually any may be used.

PLYWOOD

Exterior grades of plywood are helpful for our birdhouses.

The American Plywood Association has uniform softwood plywood grading standards that start with face grades of plywood. Face grades vary from A to C, for our purposes. A grades are unnecessary for birdhouse construction, so we'll concentrate on B and lower grades.

B-grade plywood has a less attractive face ply than A-grade. B grades are generally considered suitable where the surfaces are painted or covered with other material.

C grades are usually unsanded, and often have open spots in the face (C-C Plugged has most of those openings filled and may also be called Underlayment grade). C-C is the lowest grade of exterior plywood you can buy, and is suitable for rough work of many kinds, including sheathing. C-D is an interior rough-construction plywood made with exterior glue. Sometimes called CDX, it is not useful for permanent outdoor installation.

Oriented strand board (OSB) is wood panels made from reconstituted, mechanically oriented wood strands bonded with resin, under heat and pressure. The strands are laid up in layers, at right angles to each other. OSB may be a single panel, or the middle layer of other panels. Wafer board is a similar product that is made from wood wafers instead of strands. The wafers are not directionally oriented. Wafer board and OSB may qualify as performance boards for sheathing and various other duties. They can work well for birdhouse roofs if the roofs are painted or covered with shingles. Although the glue in these panels is waterproof, the changing size of the small pieces of wood when wetted and dried frequently mars the surface of the wood, so it's best painted or covered.

Face species for plywood are important only in how they affect your finish. Softwood plywood isn't pretty when stained, so a painted surface is best. If a natural finish is desired, low-grade solid pine is no more expensive than pine-faced plywood.

Plywood is laid up in odd-numbered plies, with thin sheets having three plies and ⅜- and ½-thick sheets having five plies. For most birdhouse uses, you won't see more than seven plies.

Various wood species are used for softwood plywood interior plies. These include some softwood and some hardwood species (although aspen, the softer maples, cottonwood, and basswood are some hardwoods usually used, beech, birch, sugar maple, lauan, and sweetgum are also sometimes used). The lower the class number, which ranges from 1 to 5, the stiffer and stronger the plywood; any plywood is strong enough for birdhouses.

Plywood serves best where panel strength is a requisite; almost any birdhouse can be made entirely of plywood, whether it is ¾-, ⅝-, ½-, or even ⅜-inch-thick plywood, oriented strand board, or wafer board. Such construction is sometimes faster and easier to use than solid wood, and may be more durable. If your birdhouse design is large enough to need glued-up boards, consider plywood.

Edging Plywoods

Covering the raw edges of plywood is one of the first signs of a high-quality woodworking job. There are a multitude of methods that can be used, some simple, some difficult.

Cutting a bevel on corners automatically covers raw edges of the visible plies. This is a simple process if your table saw is equipped with an aftermarket fence and you have an accurate blade angle setup, or if you have a specialty saw. Otherwise, it can be very difficult.

Solid-wood edging is especially good for softwood plywoods used for birdhouses. Cut it to just slightly thicker than the thickness of the plywood, and then glue it in place. Contact cement is not suitable for thicker materials such as this, so use Titebond II adhesive for its weather resistance. You will also have to apply pressure to the edging. The best method is to use edge clamps, but a tight application of masking tape or driving in a few brads also works. Brad nailers that work with air compressors make the latter technique even easier than it used to be.

Wood putty also serves as an edge filler for plywood, in cases where the edges will be painted. It is simple, fast, and inexpensive, and possibly the best approach to take for most birdhouse builders.

You may use solid-wood edging in matching or contrasting colors, as you wish. I feel walnut looks great on maple, but there is little need to get that fancy on a birdhouse, unless you desire an artistic look.

SOLID WOODS

Solid woods are sawn from a log, and planed for later use. They may or may not be kiln- or air-dried to a particular moisture content, but they are not laminate, particleboard, or any other kind of manufactured wood product.

There is a lot of misinformation given out about solid woods, including the idea that they're always better than manufactured woods, something that is not true. Plywood and other manufactured wood products are always more dimensionally stable than wide solid boards; thus, cabinets are often produced with wide parts made of plywoods or similar products, and smaller parts (frames) of solid wood. Cost is one other factor.

Softwoods are generally used as construction lumber and hardwoods for furniture and cabinetry, although, as with most generalizations, there are exceptions: pine, fir, cedar, redwood and other softwoods are often used for furniture as well for general construction.

The following chart gives an indication of basic uses of some softwoods and hardwoods, and the areas in which they are available commercially.

Opposite page and pages 12 and 13. Chart detailing uses of some soft- and hardwoods.

Wood Materials for Birdhouses

Wood Characteristics			Wood Characteristics		
Wood	*Locale*	*Characteristics*	*Wood*	*Locale*	*Characteristics*
Ash	East of the Rockies	A wood with a strong, heavy, tough grain that is straight. Sometimes substitutes for more costly oaks.	Cypress	Maryland to Texas	A water-resistant, very durable wood that may be expensive and difficult to locate.
Basswood	Eastern half of the United States	Soft, light, weak wood that shrinks considerably, has fine, even texture, works easily, and does not twist or warp.	Douglas fir	Pacific coast of United States and British Columbia	A strong, light, clear-grained, brittle wood with heartwood somewhat resistant to weathering. It is available and moderately priced, but has been rising in price in recent years.
Beech	East of Mississippi and southeastern Canada	A hard, strong, closed-grained wood that shrinks and checks considerably. It may be a light or dark red color.	Elm	East of Colorado	A wood that is heavy, hard, difficult to split and durable.
Birch	East of Mississippi, north of Gulf Coast states, southeastern Canada, and Newfoundland	A hard, durable, fine-grain wood with an even texture that works easily and takes a high polish. It is light-to-dark-reddish brown.	Hickory	Arkansas, Tennessee, Ohio, and Kentucky	A very heavy and hard wood that is the strongest and toughest of the United States hardwoods. It checks and shrinks and is difficult to work.
Butternut	Southern Canada, Minnesota, and eastern United States.	A moderately light and soft wood that is easy to work and fairly strong.			
Cherry	Eastern United States	A durable, strong, easy-to-machine furniture wood with a closed grain. It has a reddish color that darkens with age if not stained.			

Wood	Locale	Characteristics
Lignum vitae	Central America, southern Mexico	A dark greenish-brown wood, that is unusually hard, close-grained, exceptionally heavy, hard to work, and characterized by a soapy feel. Useful for mallets, etc.
Live oak	Coasts of Oregon and California, and southern Atlantic and Gulf states	A heavy, hard, strong, and durable wood that is difficult to work, but superb for small projects otherwise.
Mahogany	Honduras, Mexico, Central America, Florida, West Indies, central Africa	One of the top cabinet woods. It has an open grain, is hard and durable, does not split badly, but does check, swell, shrink, and warp slightly. It varies in color from brown to red.
Maple	All states east of Colorado, and southern Canada	A heavy, tough, strong, easy-to-work wood that is not durable. It may be costly. Rock, or sugar, maple is the hardest.
Norway pine	Great Lakes states	A light-colored wood that is moderately hard for softwood, is not durable, and is easy to work.
Poplar	Virginia, West Virginia, Kentucky, and along Mississippi Valley	A soft, cheap hardwood, good for wide boards, that rots quickly if not protected. It warps, is brittle, and has a fine texture.

Wood Characteristics

Wood	Locale	Characteristics
Red cedar	East of Colorado and north of Florida	A very light, very soft, weak, brittle wood that works easily, may be hard to find in wide boards, and is very durable.
Red oak	Virginia, West Virginia, Kentucky, Tennessee, Arkansas, Ohio, Missouri, Maryland, and parts of New York	A coarse-grained, easily warped wood that is not durable. Do not use it for doors.
Redwood	California	An ideal construction wood that shrinks and splits little, is straight-grained, is exceptionally durable, needing no finish at all, and is available in many inexpensive grades. It tends to cost more than other woods.
Spruce	New York, New England, West Virginia, Great Lakes states, Idaho, Washington, Oregon, and much of central Canada	A light, soft, fairly durable wood that is close to ideal for outdoor projects.

Wood Characteristics

Wood	Locale	Characteristics
Sugar pine	California, Oregon	A very light, soft wood that closely resembles white pine.
Walnut	Eastern half of United States, and New Mexico, Arizona, and California	A fine furniture wood, considered by many to be the ultimate one. It is coarse-grained, but takes a superb finish when its pores are filled, and it is durable, brittle, and often knotty, and has modest shrinkage.
White cedar	Eastern coast of the United States and around Great Lakes	A soft, light, durable, and close-grained wood. excellent for outdoor uses.
White oak	Virginia, West Virginia, Tennessee, Arkansas, Ohio, Kentucky, Missouri, Maryland, and Indiana	A heavy, hard, tough, and dense wood with moderately coarse grain. It is the most durable of all the United States hardwoods. Reasonably easy to work (with sharp tools), it has a tendency to shrink and crack, and may be costly in some locales.

Wood Characteristics

Wood	Locale	Characteristics
White pine	Minnesota, Wisconsin, Maine, Michigan, Idaho, Montana, Oregon, Washington, California; some stands in eastern states other than Maine	A fine-grained, easily worked wood sometimes found with a few knots. It is durable, soft, not exceptionally strong, economical, and excellent for birdhouses. It shrinks, and does not split easily.
Yellow pine	Virginia to Texas (some species classed as southern pine)	A hard, tough softwood, with a heartwood that is fairly durable. It is inexpensive and hard to nail, generally works easily, and is excellent for birdhouses. It has a variable grain and a reddish brown color and is heavy for a softwood because of its resin.

My chart doesn't include all domestic woods by any means, and makes no attempt, other than with lignum vitae, to cover foreign woods, including exotics. It doesn't seem likely that a great many people are going to be interested in the qualities of teak for use in a birdhouse. It's simply too costly. Very little walnut, cherry or maple, for that matter, is apt to be used for these projects, but for those who might want to try them, they're included in the list. If you desire more information on wood, please check *Woodworker's Guide to Selecting and Milling Wood* (Charles Self, Betterway Books, Cincinnati, 1994).

Grading Solid Woods

It's necessary to know a little about grading solid woods, so that the least costly and easiest-to-use wood with the greatest expected durability may be selected for each project.

Finish-grade lumber is used where you desire the highest-quality finish, particularly for stains and clear finishes.

Board-grade lumber is used for sheathing, subflooring, shelving, boxing, and carting in general. This grade is probably the most generally useful for projects that require boards of any kind. For our purposes, we'll consider wood boards that are nominally 1 inch thick or less.

Dimension lumber is surfaced softwood lumber used for joists, rafters, studs, and small timbers. This is the most popular type of softwood solid-wood lumber to be found these days, and, for our purposes, is available in structural light framing, light framing, stud, structural joist, and plank styles.

There is also an *appearance framing grade* of wood. *Appearance-grade* wood has a very good appearance and is very strong.

As is almost always the case, especially with smaller projects, it is a good idea to check out lumber at the lumberyard. Most yards allow you to select your own lumber, piece by piece, and that's a good thing, for some junk gets mixed in with the good wood; in some yards, some good wood gets mixed in with the junk. For birdhouse projects, such selection isn't really essential, but it can prove helpful.

HARDWOOD LUMBER

Hardwood lumber isn't as easy to come by or as easy to buy as softwood lumber. It is always virtually twice as expensive as any softwood (with the exception of redwood purchased in the east, where the transportation costs make the prices artificially high), and in the case of exotic hardwood lumber much more than twice as expensive.

With hardwood lumber generally available in four grades, selection would seem easier, but there is usually more of a problem matching grain and making sure the free-cut lengths (a length of wood without any faults in it) needed are available in such grain matches.

The specifications for most of the lumber graded by the National Hardwood Lumber Association are slightly different for each species, with the exception of the four general grades. We'll concentrate on them: FAS (Firsts and Seconds); Select; No. 1 Common; and No. 2 Com-

mon. FAS is the best and most expensive grade, where pieces should be no less than 6 inches wide and 8 feet long. At least 83⅓ percent of each board should provide clear cuttings. Selects give the same percentage of clear cutting in boards 4 inches wide and 6 feet long or longer. One face may have more defects than the other.

The two common grades should provide boards at least 3 inches wide by 4 feet long, with No. 1 Common giving 66⅔ percent clear cuttings, and No. 2 producing 50 percent clear cuttings.

WOOD DEFECTS

Examining lumber for purchase, you will note some defects that are obvious. Others may not become obvious until later, when you find internal knots and other defects that don't appear on the surface. Following is a list of defects you should be on the lookout for:

A. *Wane* is bark along the edges of the board, or missing wood along the edge of the board (usually caused by bark dropping off).

B. *Checking* is splitting of the board, usually at the ends but sometimes at other spots.

C. *Cupping* is a board warped across its width, deviating from its flatness.

D. *Warping* is a distortion of the shape of the wood, usually a combination of a linear twist and some cupping.

E. *Crook* is a form of warping, a deviation in end-to-end straightness.

F. *Crack* is a large radial check.

G. *Diamonding* is a form of warp, too, and shows square sections of the board as diamond-shaped (round sections become oval).

H. *Sap stain* is a bluish stain caused by fungi in and on the surface of the wood.

I. *Knots* are parts of branches which the expanding tree has overgrown. *Pin knots* are less than a quarter inch in diameter. A *spike knot* has been cut along its long axis, giving its exposed section a stretched appearance. *Sound knots* are solid throughout the board and show no signs of rot. *Encased*, or *black*, *knots* are knots that are loose but remain in the tree, trapped by later growth.

You can often build birdhouse projects with cutoffs from other, larger projects. This is a great way to use up what might otherwise become kindling for a fire, but give some thought to the wood being used, no matter what type. And, in each and every case, as mentioned earlier, check all dimensions on any plan before cutting multiple parts! For that matter, dry-assemble the parts and check their fit before getting started on a finished assembly in any project.

* * *

3. Fasteners for Birdhouses

Mechanical fasteners generally consist of screws and nails, with some variations. A lot of fastening today is done with air nailers, even in small projects. Brad and pneumatic finish nailers used with small (1½-horsepower or less) air compressors do a superb job of providing grip in place of clamps when you nail and glue projects. And, often, many of the finish nailers drive nails up to 2½ inches long, and do a fine job of fastening many projects together, large or small.

SCREWS

There are many types of wood screws and screw-type fasteners that can be used to fasten wood, and fasten things to wood. Those that are popular have become so for good reason. Today, new tools appear more frequently on the market; these tools bring a need for new driver shapes and different screw head designs.

The new screws are meant to be power-driven; with the array of cordless power drivers now on the market, cam-out resisting screws are needed more than ever. Cam-out is the twisting out of a screw head of the driver tip as power is applied. Square-insert screws, which resist cam-out, are being used more frequently with hand and power drivers. The standard slotted-head screw is becoming obsolete because available power in cordless driver drills is constantly being increased, and the slotted-head screw is more susceptible to cam-out. Virtually all companies sell 12-volt drill drivers. Several sell 13.2-volt models. Of those I've tried, the DeWalt model is the most powerful, but the Porter-Cable model, the Freud 13.2-volt driver, the Ryobi 12-volt driver, the Makita 12-volt model, and Sears' Craftsman all follow closely behind. The Skil Top Gun is also a fine tool, although speedier than it is powerful (I haven't had a chance to try the new model, which is supposed to be a bit more powerful). I've used the Skil FlexiCharge extensively and find it dandy for most project work, and it sells for less than $50 and weighs about ⅓ what the super power drills do (Illus. 3–1). Also, it doesn't drive screws so hard and fast it breaks boards—unless you're exceptionally careless. You can save time with cordless driver drills for some types of birdhouse assembly, but much more time is saved with pneumatic finish and brad nailers.

Screw Types

Screws may be classified as wood, lag or metal screws. If threads are used, use nut-and-bolt screws. Wood screws have round, flat, or oval heads, while metal screws have pan, flat, round, and a variety of other heads of little or no interest here. Lag screws generally have a square or hexagonal head and coarser screw threads than wood screws. They come in larger sizes. Wood screws run up to 6 inches in length and to #24 in size (the numbers refer to the diameter, but not in terms of inches in fractions.) You'll find wood screws up to about 4 or 5 inches in length and #16 in size in most hardware stores, in a number of materials. Larger sizes, and extremely small sizes such as ¼ inches × #0, #1, #2, or #3, may have to be ordered.

Illus. 3–1. The Skil Flexi-Charge drill/driver, T nuts, and square-drive machine screw inserts are one type of assembly system that can be used for birdhouses.

Wood screws are made of mild steel, solid brass, or stainless steel, and are coated or uncoated. Wood screws are used where corrosion resistance is essential; a plated zinc or galvanized coating is normally used. Stainless-steel screws are useful when corrosion problems run to extremes, such as on or around salt water, and in high-acid environments. They do not corrode much, but are the most expensive type of wood screw. Steel screws are used where strength greater than that provided by brass screws is required. Brass screws, the weakest of the three generally available wood-screw materials, are decorative and corrode very slowly. Mild steel, even zinc-plated, is the cheapest material.

Wood screws vary in length from ¼ to 6 inches. Screws that are ¼ to 1 inch long increase in length in ⅛-inch increments, while screws from 1 to 3 inches long increase in length by ¼-inch increments. Screws from 3 to 6 inches long increase in ½-inch increments. Their shaft sizes vary according to the number used to specify such a size. Shaft-size numbers are arbitrary, but become greater when the size of the screw increases.

Power-drive screws, both fine- and coarse-threaded, come in sizes somewhat different than those used for commonly available wood screws in the past (Illus. 3–2). Drive screws tend to be available in longer lengths (up to 3 inches) and with light shanks (for example, a #6, and seldom larger than a #9), where common wood screws would have thicker shanks in relation to the length (usually at least a #10 for a 3-inch length, but most often a #12 and frequently a #14).

Power-drive screws have a Phillips or a square-drive head. They are exceptionally useful for installing deck-ing, wallboard, and wall panelling of certain types, and for general light construction duties such as those involved in building birdhouses.

Screws are less economical than nails, but provide benefits for the extra cost. Their holding strength is much higher. Disassembly is easier and nondestructive, which means that you can readily set up any birdhouse for easy clean-out at the end of the season. I've reached the point where I like to use no more than three large-headed screws to install the floor, one side, or a similar part that may be easily removed so that old nesting materials can be removed (Illus. 3–3).

Screws are more work to install. For many screws, a pilot hole is needed, and for flathead wood screws, countersinking is essential. Flathead wood screws are used for decorative purposes where screws are not meant to show, and are often counterbored. The resulting hole is filled with a plug that may be flush to the surface or domed.

When drilling pilot holes in hardwood, use a drill bit at least one size less than the threads of the screw; when drilling into softwood, it should be at least two sizes less. Make the hole one-half to two-thirds as deep as the screw will sink.

Other Screw Fasteners

Machine screws are used with nuts and washers to join wood to metal or to many other materials, including wood. Machine screws come in different materials, just as do wood screws, and may be used to produce an easily assembled and disassembled project.

Among the popular holders for machine screws are T

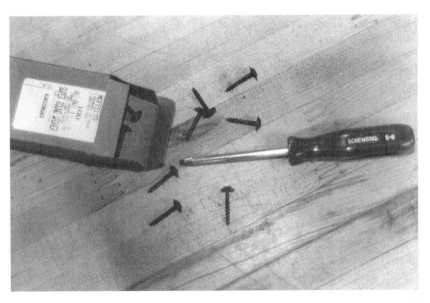

Illus. 3–2. McFeely's square-drive screws are ideal for hand and power use.

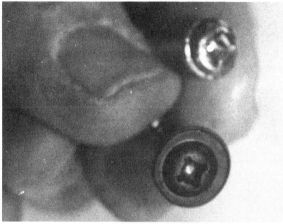

Illus. 3–3. Washers with super-round heads are less destructive to wood that those with standard washer heads.

nuts and brass-screw inserts. A T nut is a type of nut that fits into a drilled hole in one wood surface. It is set in place and then tapped down so that the teeth in the upper ring grip. The screw is then run into the T nut as if it were an ordinary nut, allowing assemblies to be mated. The screw and T nut can be easily disassembled. T nuts and brass-screw inserts are useful means of providing removable bases for birdhouses so that they can be cleaned out.

Brass-screw inserts work in a manner similar to T nuts as far as holding power goes, but you insert them by screwing them into a hole drilled to size. The inserts have coarse male threads on their outside and finer female threads on their inside. They are screwed into the holes—their top is slotted to accept a standard flat-blade screwdriver tip of the appropriate size. The insert is turned down until its top is flush with the board, and then a brass or steel machine screw is driven into its internal threads. For insert fasteners, you may use knurled screws. Knurled screws are decorative, but also ease disassembly because no tool is needed to install or remove them.

NAILS

The nail is still the most useful mechanical fastener around. Though it is the least strong fastener, it costs very little and can be installed easily and quickly. The drop in cost of home-shop air compressors and the quantity of air-powered finish and brad nailers available on the market have helped nails retain their usefulness in the small shop.

Iron nails go back as far as the Roman occupation of Great Britain and quite probably before that. Roman nails

were forged, creating differences in shape caused by manufacture, but in general were similar to today's wire nail.

Cut nails superseded forged nails in the late 1700s and early 1800s. Early cut nails had handmade heads, but by about 1830 the entire nail was cut by machine. Cut nails certainly provide an unusual look for birdhouses, and have greater holding strength than common wire nails.

Nails are sized by the penny (abbreviated "d"), a method once used by manufacturers to determine how many cents 100 nails would cost. Given inflation over the past century, the actual cost changed rapidly, but the sizing system has been retained, still ranging from 2d to 60d, although many makers prefer now to sell nails by length and weight.

Nails under 2d or 1 inch are classed as brads; those over 60d (6 inches) are classified as spikes.

Common nails are used for general-purpose nailing, from framing work to some types of flooring installation. Their shank styles differ; greater holding power is found with deformed shanks such as ring and screw shanks. They are available coated, and the nails may often be hardened. Common nails also come in aluminum as well as galvanized coating for outdoor uses.

Finishing nails are slim, nearly headless nails in sizes ranging from the 1-inch brad finishing nail on up to 16d (3½ inches) and beyond. They come in clean mild steel, galvanized, and hot-dipped galvanized, and are used because their small heads are easily set (with a nail set) below a board's surface, where a touch of putty eliminates any nailed look.

PNEUMATIC NAILERS AND STAPLERS

I've managed to get my hands on many of today's finish and brad nailers, in an effort both to speed up my work and research them for your possible use. I can't make the statement that they don't cost much more than a good hammer, although good hammers have increased a great deal in price in the past few years. Still, there's a goodly number of one and one-and-a-half horsepower air compressors available, some weighing barely over 40 pounds, and the competition is intense among the manufacturers of compressors and their accessories (Illus. 3–4).

For rapid assembly of many birdhouses, give thought to air-driven brad nailers that use fasteners up to 1¼ inches in length. These easy-to-use tools are now about three times the price of a good hammer (if you've already got a compressor and hose, you can quickly set up). Speed is increased incredibly, and the brad and most

Illus. 3–4. The DeVilbiss 40-pound, one-horsepower compressor can be easily lifted and moved around, yet it drives air nailers quite nicely.

Illus. 3–5. I've used both Campbell-Hausfeld and DeVilbiss brad nailers extensively during the past couple of years, and now insist on having one around at all times.

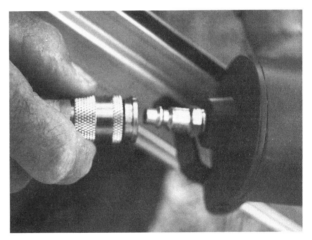

Illus. 3–6. Always remember to detach a pneumatic nailer's air hose when clearing jams or reloading.

finish nailers work exceptionally well even with air compressors that have only a ¾-horsepower motor. Finish nailers are more expensive, but take nails up to 2½ inches long, allowing a range of nails suitable for almost any fastening use where an unheaded nail makes sense (Illus. 3–5).

All the air-driven fasteners I've seen are galvanized or otherwise coated, so are suitable for use on outdoor and indoor projects. The brads range in length from ¾ to 1¼ inches, and the finishing nails from 1 to 2½ inches.

All the air-driven nailers I've worked with are easy to use, drive their fasteners accurately and quickly, and can be adjusted (at the compressor) for setting the depth of the nail head. Some have a flip-up gate at their nose. These are extremely useful in clearing stoppages, but you *must* remember to detach the air hose when lifting the gate. It is extremely dangerous otherwise (Illus. 3–6).

I can honestly say that on every recent birdhouse I or Bobby Weaver has built, we have used either air finish nailers or brad nailers. The increase in speed and the lack of bounce when driving nails make even odd shapes easy to put together. Anyone making large numbers of small projects like birdhouses owes it to himself or herself to investigate the cost and usefulness of such tools.

* * *

4. Hand Tools for Birdhouse Projects

As far as possible, the projects in this book are designed to be built with fairly simple tools that most homeowners or woodworkers with small shops have. There's little that cannot be completed with a circular saw, a bayonet saw, and a few other hand tools. Much of the cutting will be easier with a band saw, a table saw, a radial arm saw, and accessories, some of which are described in this chapter. Certain pieces will be easier to trim with a scroll saw and a router, but most may also be cut with a bayonet saw or a hand scroll saw. Below I describe the assortment of hand tools that will be helpful.

MEASURING TOOLS

The basic tools for any woodworking project are those with which you transfer measurements from plans to wood. Accurate transfer of the measurements is essential in ensuring the ease and dependability of the construction.

Measurements are taken with several tools, among which are folding rules and measuring tapes. For tighter spots, and greater accuracy, there are also calipers. Many calipers also have rod-style depth gauges, which are a great help when making inside measurements of some joints (mortises, dowel hole depths, etc.).

Measuring tapes come in a great many lengths and a number of widths. For most project purposes, lengths above a dozen feet aren't necessary, although they may be handy for finding a location for various birdhouses and posts. When buying a measuring tape, go for the absolute best you can afford, with the widest possible tape. The wider the tape, the stronger and stiffer it is; thus, the longer it lasts (and the easier it is to read).

Folding rules usually come in 6- and 8-foot lengths. The good ones have brass hardware, and some models offer a sliding brass extension that also serves to help take depth measurements. Get a good one.

Flat rules are available in metal and wood. Metal rules are more durable and need less care, but also tend to lose precision more often with slight temperature changes. In most cases when working with wood that's not a problem, because the loss isn't great enough to affect the required accuracy.

The basics of measuring are quite simple and don't need to be described, except that you should remember to tilt the tape or rule when making a mark on the workpiece. Such a tilt ensures that the appropriate mark is on the surface, and not on a piece of the tape or on the rule.

Marks can be made with standard pencils, carpenter's pencils, or scribes. While a scribe is the most precise marker, the thick lead of a carpenter's pencil can be made nearly as precise, and the mark is more easily seen. Simply cut the pencil down with a knife to form a wedge shape, and then sand the point sharp; I cheat and use a power sander to do the job. If light is good in your shop area, go ahead and use the scribe—it very seldom needs sharpening and gives a really sharp working line.

SQUARES

The squares used for small woodworking projects are the try square, the combination square, the speed square, and the framing square. All come in different sizes and types, so there is almost always the proper square for the job.

Try squares offer a basic and reliable 90-degree angle setting, with a not-so-precise 45-degree setting on many handles. The try square tends to be the most precise type of square because its handle and tongue are solidly held together.

Combination squares serve various functions for most people, and succeed reasonably well as an adjustable square, for both 90 and 45 degrees, and as a marker. As a level, they fail—the bubble takes too much of a beating to retain accuracy for long. The try square is more accurate than the combination square at 90 degrees, but is not as convenient. Setting the combination square blade at a specific distance allows use of the scribe often included in the handle to mark that distance on a board.

Framing squares have many try-square features, but are larger (the standard size is 24 × 16 inches, including the blade and tongue). I suggest a stainless-steel framing square, because the aluminum squares nick too easily and the mild-steel versions rust too easily, unless given a black-powder coating. You might want to get an extra framing square and fasten a carefully fabricated hardwood handle at the tongue end. This provides you with a superb 24-inch-long try square, although Stanley now makes a contractor's 16-inch combination square that is super for wider surfaces.

The quality of your work depends on the quality of the squares and how well they're used. A basic shop needs at least one good combination and one good try square.

HANDSAWS

Saws are the primary cutting tools for woodworking. For our projects, the following saws are needed: a 10-point panel saw; a 12-inch or larger backsaw; and a coping, or scroll, saw. If you use metal or harder plastics, you might wish to get a hacksaw. For rougher cuts, one of the newer hard-tooth handsaws, with eight points per inch, cuts quickly and neatly. These are the only low-cost handsaws I've ever seen that are worth the money (Illus. 4–1 and 4–2).

A mitre box is also handy. There are a number of different versions, but the Jorgenson power mitre box, with its changeable blade, cut-depth regulator, and compound mitre feature is very useful. I prefer sliding-compound mitre boxes over others. They are costly, but do a super job and have helped change the way carpenters work (for example, it's possible to make cutoffs with just a single mark on the wood, with no need to use a square, in most cuts of over 10 inches at 90 degrees with most sliding compound mitre boxes). The number of power mitre boxes on the market increases each year, with Makita recently adding a 12-inch sliding compound mitre box.

When using any handsaw, it's essential you use it properly: Start a cut on the waste side of the cutting line,

Illus. 4–1. Freud's finish saw is not low-cost, but works beautifully and leaves a clean-cut line.

Illus. 4–2. Freud's Gent saw is the shortest backsaw around and is very handy for making straight cuts in narrow stock without using a mitre box.

guiding the saw with your thumb knuckle against the side of the blade until the teeth bite into the wood. Cut with the handle at a comfortable angle, generally between 45 and 60 degrees.

Saw care is simple. Make sure the blade won't strike the ground, or other objects, under the wood being cut. Make sure there are no nails in the wood being cut. Do not force a saw that twists in a cut. Back off, clean the blade, and try again. Often, the saw twists because the board is twisting, too. Whenever possible, handsaws should be hung up, instead of being laid down. Keep the blade lightly oiled and free of gum and pitch buildup.

HAMMERS

Hammers are available in many styles and sizes, but for birdhouse projects a good-quality 16-ounce, curved-claw hammer is suitable. Curved-claw hammers have better balance than rip-claw hammers, and a 16-ounce head is a good choice between lightweight and heavyweight (head weights vary from 10 ounces to 28 ounces). For small birdhouse projects, get a 13-ounce model, too.

Hammer handles are made from fibreglass, or solid or tubular steel. There are advantages to each material: Wood costs a bit less, fibreglass is easiest on the hand and forearm, and steel is strongest. A fibreglass handle is probably the best for most uses, but if you like tubular or solid steel, or wood, all are fine. Recently, some companies have been producing solid-steel-handled hammers, with the old Estwing pattern as a base but with other advanced technological features, and I find that I like a number of those quite a lot, although in earlier years I always used hammers with fibreglass handles (Illus. 4–3). Make sure that any hammer handle is securely attached to its head, a feature of all good hammers.

Head weight is a personal choice, with standard weights ranging from 13 ounces (useful for much storage project work) to a standard 16-ounce head, and up to 28-ounce monsters with longer handles. Birdhouses do not require a hammer head weighing over 16 ounces.

Soft-faced hammers come in many versions, from rawhide- to plastic-faced. Rubber mallets are also available. For assembly uses, any of these hammers may prove handy. I like weighted rawhide heads for some uses, and basic rawhide heads for others. I also keep an array of Plumb plastic heads available—these are the least complex to select, generally, so I have several. I use several Stanley plastic-handled hammers and their rubber mallet frequently in project assembly. Not long ago, I got hold of a sculptor's mallet (great for driving chisels)

Illus. 4–3. Vaughan & Bushnell's 10-ounce Little Pro hammer is amazingly easy to use for small projects.

and a round beech-head mallet, which works well for driving chisels and for knocking tight joints together—or apart.

SCREWDRIVERS

Screwdrivers come in different styles to match specific screw heads. Select a good-quality screwdriver that will match the screw heads you are working with. Good screwdrivers will have handles that fit your hand well, and blades made of alloys that last. Their tips are machined clean and neat. Screwdrivers that handle the best are those with wedge-shaped handles that spread out more as they reach the shank.

Remember that when using square-drive screws, you'll need square-drive screwdrivers, which are available from a number of sources in all the sizes (#0, #1, #2) required for birdhouse assembly.

STAPLERS

Staplers are useful for attaching fabrics, and light woods to heavier woods. Recent use of air-powered staplers has moved me completely away from hand and electric staplers, except for hammer-style staplers. Air-powered staplers are simpler and seem more efficient, and are less likely to jam than electric versions. Hand staplers are a great deal of work when you do much stapling, eventually providing a really solid case of hand cramps.

For birdhouses, you may wish to staple screens over vents, but otherwise there simply isn't much use for any kind of stapler, unless you decide to do assembly with a small finish stapler. These staplers use up to 1¼-inch-long staples and do a superb job of attaching materials up to ½ inch thick.

PAINTBRUSHES

A quick note on paintbrushes: For the construction of the projects in this book, I used 3M's disposable brushes, in 1-, 2-, and 3-inch widths. They are exceptionally useful for paint and enamel finishes, but are not particularly effective with clear finishes. Their bristles are not nearly fine enough to give a smooth, bubble-free clear finish coat. Stick with super-quality natural bristles for clear finishes and use the cheaper brushes elsewhere.

*   *   *

5. Power Tools

ELECTRIC DRILLS

You no longer need an outlet when using an electric drill because cordless drills that are powerful and convenient to use are now readily available. Some models are extremely powerful, have durable batteries, and also offer a quick-charge feature. Top-grade cordless drills are often sold with an extra battery pack included, which means you can work all day long if you want to. For standard birdhouse work, 7.2- and 9.6-volt models are close to ideal, and both Skil and Black & Decker now have lighter weight models that take what might be termed stackable battery packs, which means that the same packs are useful in different combinations for different tools. These lightweight cordless drills are easier to handle and often simplify jobs such as driving screws in thin wood, where a heavy-duty drill may provide enough power to crack the wood.

Recently, I worked with a whole bunch of heavy-duty cordless drills and enjoyed using them, a real change from my start with such drills over 15 years ago. When I bought my first cordless drill, the politest comment I made after a week's use was that I was not happy with the tool. It was a single unit—no detachable battery—that agonized its way through about eighteen or twenty ⅛-inch holes in wet oak planking after being on charge for 16 hours. And it was very expensive.

Today's assortment of heavy-duty cordless drills, driver drills, and hammer drills is also expensive, but you get much more for your money. I no longer remember how much voltage the battery in that old drill packed, but today's versions range from 7.2 volts on up to 14.4 volts in the newest, heaviest-duty DeWalt model.

The 16-hour charge has been obsolete for some time now. The fastest readily available charger will charge your battery pack in *10 minutes*! The slowest of the top-grade models will charge your battery pack in one hour. Even low-cost consumer models give you a charge overnight, and many do so in three hours.

You need to determine if a cordless drill is worth buying instead of a corded drill—or in addition to a corded drill (Illus. 5–1 and 5–2). For sheer drilling power, the corded drill will always win. For ease of setup, transportability, and general usefulness in light-to-medium work, the corded drill is no match for cordless units.

Cordless drills are exceptionally helpful where electric power isn't available, which is why they are so popular for outdoor use. They are also very handy indoors. They are a delight to use around the shop because of the lack of a need for a cord, their ability to function around damp locations with fewer precautions, and for other reasons.

Most cordless drills also offer keyless chucks, which speed up work considerably. Such chucks work on a simple reverse twist to hold the implements and accessories in place, and do almost as good a job as a keyed chuck (Illus. 5–3).

Illus. 5–1. Makita's 12-volt cordless drill handles very nicely and has great power.

Illus. 5–2. DeWalt's 14.4-volt cordless drill is very powerful and is the heaviest cordless I've ever used, although Porter-Cable's 12-volt version comes close (and is also very powerful).

Illus. 5–3. This 12-volt keyless-chuck cordless drill is being used to easily drill a 2-inch hole saw through redwood.

Maintenance and Safety Precautions

Battery-powered drills and other tools require some specific precautions. They are as follow:
1. Keep the tools, chargers and batteries dry, and recharge them only in a cool, dry area.
2. Do *not* operate cordless tools in a flammable atmosphere, or around flammable materials. They are still driven by electric motors that spark just like their corded equivalents.
3. Unlike unplugged corded tools, cordless tools are basically always ON, unless you take necessary precautions. Lock the switch in the OFF position or remove the battery pack when storing tools. Always make sure the tool is locked in the OFF position or the battery pack is removed when installing cutters and similar accessories.
4. As with all tools, keep cordless driver drills, hammer drills, and other drills out of the reach of children and untrained adults.
5. When the battery packs do give out, recycle them properly. Many communities do not want such items in landfills or in general trash-disposal areas, because nicad batteries may explode if immersed in water or burned. Return the old battery pack to your dealer, where you'll need to go to buy the new pack anyway. The dealer returns it to the distributor, who then properly recycles the old unit.

Cordless 12-volt drills can do a full day of normal work on two battery packs. In one single day, I managed to position, drill pilot holes for, and drive 3-inch screws to hold down the flooring for a 14- × 16-foot deck with two drills of different voltage. I used the less-powerful 13.2-volt drill to drill the ⅛-inch pilot holes; one battery pack was used, and there was still plenty of charge remaining after about nine hours' work. The second, 14.4-volt drill was used on low speed to drill in the screws, and still had charge remaining in its second battery pack at day's end. I do not know exactly how many screws I drove, nor how much difference there would have been using different woods, a different pattern of screw thread, etc. Suffice it to say, I worked as long as I could in very hot weather that is not good for the battery packs, and both drills performed perfectly.

Selecting a Cordless Drill

When getting a cordless drill, consider the following features:

1. Its *total power.* Cordless drills range in power from 7.2 volts up to 14.4 volts. Prices rise relative to the voltage, and remember that a drill with 7.2 volts is often sufficient for drilling and driving screws in birdhouses (Illus. 5–4), although if you use as much oak as I have for these projects, you'll welcome drills with greater power.
2. Whether it has a keyless chuck. A drill with a keyless chuck will make lost chuck keys a thing of the past and provide a quick way to change from drill to driver and back to drill.

Illus. 5–4. Skil's Flexi-Charge 7.2-volt cordless drill drove a lot of screws for the birdhouses in this book, and never faltered. Such lighter-weight, lower-cost drills handle easily and are very useful.

3. Whether it has two speed ranges. This is an essential, except for the truly unusual drill (Porter-Cable offers a single-speed, ½-inch chuck model that has just a moderately low speed and no high speed, but works in most situations).
4. Its charging capacity. A one-hour charging capacity is now the norm.
5. Whether it has extra battery packs. Some units come with two packs standard. Jim Ray at McFeely's has informed me they're selling the DeWalt 14.4-volt cordless drill with a second battery pack for slightly more than the cost of a single-pack model. A second pack is almost essential for very heavy work, but for most day-to-day work it's not really critical. For birdhouses a 14.4-volt drill with a second battery pack is excessive, but a lot

depends on what other work you plan to do when you choose such a tool.

6. How the drill handles. Each drill handles a little differently than the others. Some battery packs are heavier than others and are inserted differently. The shapes of the drill handles also vary. If possible, try out any unit before buying it. If you can't, make sure there's a liberal return policy.

Cordless drills do almost every kind of drilling, and anything else a corded drill does, including running hole saws and similar accessories. I started out hating cordless drills over 15 years ago. Now, I won't be without at least two (Illus. 5–5).

Illus. 5–5. This DeWalt cordless drill handles ⅛-inch pilot holes easily.

Illus. 5–6. The Porter-Cable T-handle, ⅜-inch-chuck corded drill is a great handling drill.

STANDARD ELECTRIC DRILLS

Standard electric drills come in many versions and chuck sizes. Select one that is durable and powerful. Drills are one tool where it doesn't pay to buy cheaply, since inexpensive models don't have many features and have a short life. For most purposes, a ⅜-inch chuck electric drill, with a variable speed and a reversible motor that draws over 3.5 amperes, works well. It should also have at least an 8-foot cord and brushes that can be replaced easily (Illus. 5–6).

POWER SAWS

Power saws provide great versatility in cutting. Below I describe some of the more versatile and helpful table saws.

Table Saws

Table saws are probably the most versatile power saw. They come in a wide range of types, sizes and styles; some are light enough to be moved easily from one job site to another, while others are not easily moved at all. What was once my main table saw weighs upwards of 750 pounds, and is not meant to be portable. It is a Delta 1½-horsepower Unisaw that by itself weighs over 400 pounds, while the Excalibur rip fence and sliding table add the rest of the weight. These two accessories increase its usefulness greatly.

Selecting a Table Saw

Selecting a table saw for one's own use is not a simple job because of the wide variety on the market. Models can accept blades that range in diameter from 4 to 14 inches, and can vary in power from a fraction of one horsepower to three-phase multi-horsepower. It is a rare small shop that requires three-phase electrical power. That is primarily for industrial needs and is found mostly in saws with 5 horsepower or more.

A table saw with a 1-to-3 horsepower motor will probably serve your needs, but more important than horsepower is the quality of the saw itself (Illus. 5–7). Tolerances need to be tight, the table precisely machined, and the various adjusters well made. The mitre slots must be precise, and the rip fence well made. Both the mitre gauge and the rip fence may be replaced with accessories such as the Excalibur units mentioned above, but remember that such units cost hundreds of dollars. They expand the capabilities of most table saws, but also eliminate portability.

Illus. 5–7. Bench-top table saws are the only power saw that's needed for birdhouse projects. (Photo courtesy of Sears, Roebuck, & Co.)

The heavier and more powerful the table saw, the less portable and the more accurate it is. Plenty of contractor's saws are both powerful and accurate. Light production saws are heavier and more accurate. If precise cuts are of great importance but portability is also necessary, consider buying a second lightweight saw. There are a number of lightweight 8- and 10-inch table saws that can almost be tucked under one's arm and carted off. Several of these offer surprising cutting accuracy (Illus. 5–8).

Grooving and Dadoing

Grooves and dadoes differ in only one way: Grooves are made with the grain of the wood, while dadoes are made against, or across, the grain of the wood. Dado sets are stacked blade assemblies that give a wider kerf, or cut (Illus. 5–9). The outer blades are similar to standard saw blades, while the inner, or chipper, blades commonly have only two teeth, located at opposing sides of the blade. The chipper blades clean out the area between the outer blades, producing a set-width groove or dado.

Other forms of dado sets exist. These are usually single or dual blade wobbler units. The one or two blades in the tool are set to wobble at a maximum specified distance, producing a cut of the same size as the wobble. Such dado sets tend to leave more material in the bottom of the grooves than do standard sets, but also tend to be faster and easier to set up. As always, you have a trade-

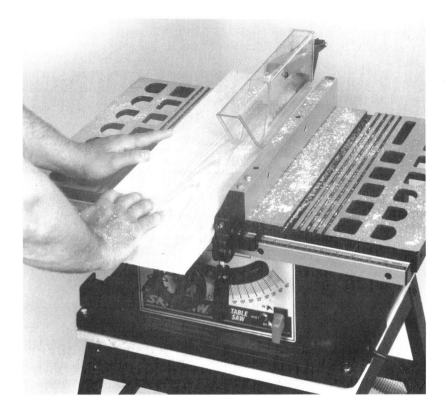

Illus. 5–8. Lightweight table saws can easily make rip cuts in lighter-bodied woods. (Photo courtesy of S-B Power Tools Corp.)

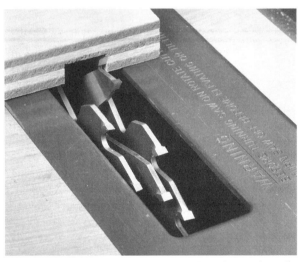

Illus. 5–9. Get a good dado set. A dado set is only needed for one of the projects in this book, but these blades are supremely useful tools for all manner of woodworking.

off: a fast setup versus more time needed to clean up the groove so the joint will fit properly. I don't like and don't use wobbler blades.

Groove and dado joints are useful for setting in shelves in cabinetry, and in cases where any shelves and dividers do not need to be adjustable for height. They are much stronger than butt joints and are neater looking and provide a really different look in some birdhouse designs.

Dado blades are useful for other types of cut. The rabbet cut is one. Rabbet cuts are channels cut into the wood, into which another piece of wood (or other material) fits to produce a rabbet joint. A rabbet cut is set up along the rip fence, leaving no lip on the cut. I prefer to work with an auxiliary fence when cutting rabbets, reducing the chance of cutting into my expensive Excalibur aluminum fence with the carbide tip of the dado blade. Use a straight piece of wood for the auxiliary fence. Attach it with screws through the factory holes in the aluminum fence (if there are no holes, drill two). Position the auxiliary fence on the table, but not so tightly against it that the aluminum fence won't move with it in place. Now, cut a relief arch in the fence facing. This arch will need to be different depths for different cuts, so start with a slight cut about two-thirds the depth of the facing width (if you used a ¾-inch-thick board, cut in about ½ inch). Raise the blade slowly to increase the depth of the relief arch to a maximum height of ¾ to 1 inch.

Mitre and Butt Joints

The *mitre joint* is a variation of the butt joint in that the pieces are cut in a true mitre at 45-degree angles and butted together and fastened in place. It is useful for picture frames, door and window moulding, and similar objects. Mitre joints are also used when working with plywood because they leave only the surface of the plywood showing, not the underlying plies. Thus, the mitre joint is a cabinetry joint used for both mouldings and frame carcass construction, but it's also useful for adding a decorative touch to birdhouses.

Butt joints are the most common joints used for woodwork. They are readily produced on a table saw both across and with the grain. Crosscuts are cuts made across the grain. The table saw is not the best tool for creating smooth crosscuts. The radial arm saw is better at this particular job but is limited in crosscut capacity. My Delta 12-inch radial arm saw, for example, has a crosscut capacity in ¾-inch material of only 16 inches (it will cut only 14 inches in thicker material). To get really decent crosscuts, it's necessary to use industrial-strength radial arm saws, such as Delta's 18-inch radial arm saw (and you won't like the cost of the saw and its blades).

For most common widths of crosscut, the radial arm saw tends to be superior to the table saw, *unless* you manage to use one of the versions of sliding tables now made for table saws.

Rip cuts, made with the grain, are truly the table saw's forte; long butt joints can be produced quite well. A decent set of hold-downs and featherboards help to maintain cut evenness, while a top-quality rip blade will provide a good glue line.

For long rip cuts, use a rip blade; combination blades are fine for shorter rip cuts but are not suitable for extensive rips in quality hardwoods. If the wood is thick, feed the workpiece fairly fast. If using an underpowered saw on very heavy wood (oak, maple, etc.), feed the workpiece much more slowly. The best approach is to feed as fast as the saw will safely accept the wood.

In order to feed rapidly, you must use a good rip blade. My preference runs to 24-tooth carbide-tipped blades with an alternate top bevel grind and a hook of about 20 degrees (these blades are similar to many combination blades, except for the hook angle). Crosscut blades have much less hook angle, often as little as 7 degrees, while combination blades will have about double the angle. Virtually all the blades have an alternate top bevel grind, though. For rougher work, a blade with 18 teeth (the number of teeth cited are for a 10-inch blade) and a flat top grind work well.

Regardless of the brand and type of blade used, keep it free of gum. Gum drags the blade, reduces available power, and tends to burn and discolor the wood. There are degumming solutions on the market, most of which are too costly. The simplest and cheapest way of removing gum is to spray the blade with any good oven cleaner. Wipe it down with a rag or damp sponge, after the appropriate soaking time. Wipe on a light coat of oil or silicone lubricant afterwards, and make your first cut in a foot-long piece of scrap stock (to get rid of excess lubricant that might ruin a finish or foul a glue line).

Band Saw

Other tools can be used for cutting that give a rougher joint than a table saw but can be used more quickly. One other stationary saw—the band saw—will do almost everything the table saw will do, with little or no danger of kickback (the prime drawback of table saws, and a function of blade design and rotation that cannot be totally eliminated), and with great ease on jobs the table saw cannot do at all well, such as cutting curves.

The band saw is a popular home-shop tool (Illus.

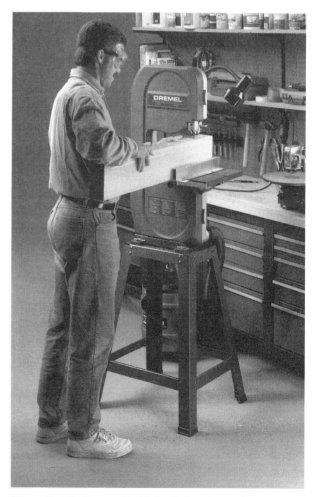

Illus. 5–10. Dremel's 10-inch band saw is powerful enough to cut wood this thick.

5–10), even though setting up one of the cheaper models can take a lot of work. At the same time, instructions on tuning a band saw go as far as to use pitch (sound) tuning techniques to get proper blade tension, but these aren't much help to those of us with little music education or a tin ear. There remains the old standby of simply measuring the tautness of the blade with thumb pressure or a tension gauge. Bobby Weaver uses his very old Craftsman model, which is finely tuned.

Newer-model bench-top band saws are much more powerful and better made than those in existence even a couple of years ago. Dremel (Illus. 5–11), Ryobi, Skil, Delta and a few others make such bench-top saws, and I'd suggest you check out one or two before completing any band-saw purchase. Many have unusual features. A hex wrench is used to track the blade on the Ryobi band saw (Illus. 5–12). The Dremel saw has two speeds. It is heavy for a bench-top model, is fairly costly, and from my testing appears to be well worth the price. It has a motor rated at ½ horsepower, higher than those on standard bench tops, and requires a minimum overall tune-up before giving clean cuts.

Band saws differ from table saws in that the blade does not spin, but rotates around two—or, in some models, three—wheels, and passes through a set of

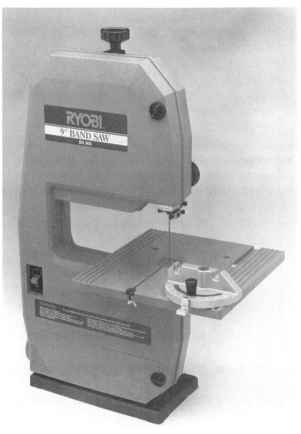

Illus. 5–12. The Ryobi 9-inch band saw does a fine job, and has a novel blade-adjusting method, in which a hex key is used. Blade changing is also very fast.

guides held above the work and table (Illus. 5–13 and 5–14). The blade is endless, that is, is a welded loop, and may vary in width from ⅛ inch to as much as 3 inches on band saws used for resawing operations (resawing is the procedure of ripping a board through its tallest dimension, to get two thinner boards).

There are also three-wheel band saws available. These offer greater throat depth, for increased saw size and power, but also provide some problems because most are lower-cost saws that do not have necks strong enough to withstand as much flexing as is needed. Basically, that means the saw is going to be less accurate than most two-wheeled models. Also, the blade has to make another turn, and all the turns are on a tighter radius than those made with a similarly sized two-wheeled saw, so blade breakage is a little more frequent. If you can find an old Inca or other sturdy three-wheeled band saw, use it. Otherwise, consider buying a two-wheeler.

Band saws can readily be used as the only saw in a shop, doing everything the table or radial arm saw will do

Illus. 5–11. The Dremel 10-inch band saw adjusts quickly and easily for bevel cuts.

Illus. 5–13. The Delta 12-inch band saw is a classic.

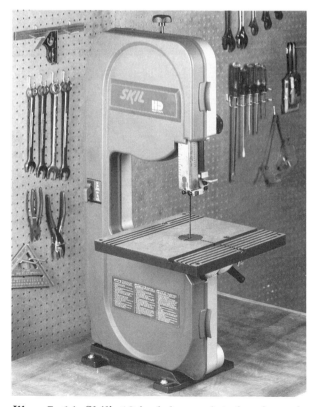

Illus. 5–14. Skil's 10-inch heavy-duty band saw is very similar to the Dremel model.

except dadoing, grooving, and cutting moulding. Certainly, I'd recommend either a band saw or a scroll saw for any shop, and suggest you start looking at the lower-cost models such as the Dremel, AMT, Craftsman, or others before investing in the more expensive ones such as Delta, RBI, Hegner, and Excalibur.

Circular Saws

Circular saws are primarily used in construction work to make mitre and butt joints. Their accuracy depends on both experience and the use of jigs to assist in the cut. It also depends on the quality of the saw itself and on the quality and sharpness of the blade.

A carbide-tipped blade is the best type of blade to use. When cutting old wood or wood that might have nails embedded in it, however, use a standard steel blade designed for cutting flooring. Nails when struck sometimes dislodge carbide tips and send them flying, an experience far better learned about in books than experienced. You can use a combination blade for general use; this minimizes changing blades, using two saws, or using a rip or cutoff blade when making both rip and crosscuts. For extra-smooth rip or crosscuts, use the appropriate blade. For the best mitres, use a top-grade planer combination blade.

When selecting a circular saw, you have a very wide range of brands and sizes to choose from. Porter-Cable offers two small units, one a 6-inch saw that works on full-sized lumber. Skil carries a 10-inch saw and a variety of popular 7¼ and 8¼-inch saws that set the industry standard. Black & Decker's new Quantum saws are nicely made consumer-plus saws (one grade up from consumer), and DeWalt's drop-foot 7¼-inch saw works nicely, as do the Makita, Ryobi, and Craftsman brands. The Porter-Cable models are pro-grade and currently have magnesium base plates. I recently spent a day with one of these saws and discovered that all that super-lightweight metal really does reduce the saw's weight enough to cut down on arm weariness.

The circular saw is a basic power saw that provides good general service. The pro saws are more accurate than the consumer models and considerably more costly, while their actual accuracy depends in large part on the skill of the user.

The rip guide, a feature often ignored on circular saws, provides an excellent base for long rips. It adjusts to allow the appropriate cutoff of material with the grain, but is not useful for cross-grain cuts. Easily used, the guide shaft slides into the slots on the saw's base, and the screw, or screws, are tightened once the distance is set. Guide the saw on the outside edge of the work and make the cut.

For deeper rip cuts and for crosscuts, a guide board is needed. Go to a lumberyard and have them cut you a piece of ¼-inch-thick tempered hardboard about a foot wide and 5–10 feet long (depending on the lengths of the cuts you expect to need; you may wish to make several of these guides in different lengths). To that tempered hardboard, glue and screw a ½-inch-thick × 4-inch-wide board that is as straight as possible. Fasten it along the long side, flush with one long edge of the thin board.

The last step in preparing the jig is simple. Set the jig in place, after measuring the width of your saw base plate to the blade, and clamp it on the material to be cut. Cut both the jig and the material. After this, measure the material and place the jig so that the cutoff edge is at the edge of where the cut will be—assuming you always use the same circular saw with this jig (mark both the jig and saw that are used together, if you have more than one circular saw).

Power Mitre Saws

Power mitre saws are a more complex but, in some ways, easier-to-use form of circular saw (Illus. 5-15–5-17). There are many models available with different features, including two DeWalt 12-inch models, a Sears Craftsman 8¼-inch sliding compound-mitre saw, one Ryobi 10-inch compound-mitre saw and one 8½-inch sliding compound-mitre version, and a Porter-Cable 10-inch Laser Loc model that uses laser beam guidelines for cuts. You can use your thumb or forefinger to easily move the markings of the cut line on the Laser Loc model from one side

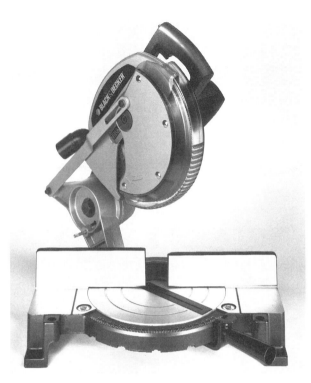

Illus. 5–16. Black & Decker's new 10-inch mitre saw provides good power at a moderate cost.

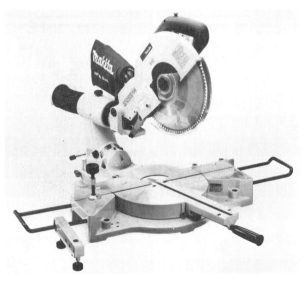

Illus. 5–17. The Makita slide dual compound saw is truly a standout mitre saw, but is very expensive.

of the blade to the other. Skil has a 10-inch mitre saw that is sturdy, durable, and probably the least costly of the saws described. Makita's newest 12-inch sliding compound-mitre saw has set the industry standard in terms of price and performance.

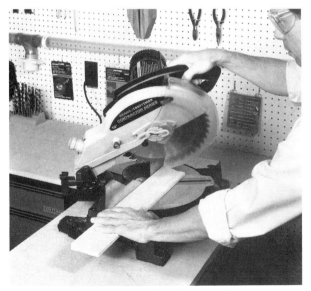

Illus. 5–15. The Sears Craftsman 12-inch compound mitre saw is moderate in cost and high in power.

Power Tools

How Valuable are Power Mitre Saws?

What do power mitre saws do for the woodworker? With the proper saw setup (mainly, support for longer boards so they don't twist and lift the saw off the worktable or jam against the blade), power mitre saws speed work and make it easier to make straight crosscuts. Much lumber doesn't make it to the shop with square ends, so a power mitre saw set up to handle the work can shave the end of every piece, ensuring that you work from a square starting point.

Cutting mitres is simpler with this type of saw than any other. Although you can line up the cuts as easily with a hand mitre saw, handsaw, or circular saw as you can with a power mitre saw, a power mitre saw cuts more easily than the hand mitre or handsaw and more accurately than a handsaw or circular saw. It is also much easier, with a power mitre saw, to slice off less than a blade's width at a time, shaving the edge to trim-fit parts perfectly.

Chop Saws

Straight mitre saws are also known as chop saws, because they make their cuts in a downward, chopping motion, with the blade and motor unit suspended from a single pivot at the rear of the tool's table. The mitre saw pivots in a single arc, with the blade remaining vertical. Skil offers a 15-ampere, 10-inch mitre saw (rated at three horsepower) that cuts a full $3\frac{1}{2}$ inches deep over a $4\frac{1}{4}$-inch width. That means it will end-cut a 4 × 4 at both 90 and 45 degrees, making it very versatile for everything from moulding work to deck building. The unit has an optional clamp, extensions, and stop, which are always handy items. Black & Decker's 10-inch mitre saw is a two-horsepower model that only weighs 26 pounds, a strong point in its favor if you move around a lot while working on projects or if you have a small shop and have to set up and take down a mitre saw several times in a week.

Porter-Cable's Laser Loc is a 10-inch, 13-ampere straight mitre saw. Classed as an industrial model, as are all of Porter-Cable's tools, the Laser Loc looks very reliable and durable. As already mentioned, the Laser Loc has laser-beam guidelines that provide an accurate marking of the cut line, on either side of the blade, to keep you from having to almost literally stick your nose on the work as the cut begins (this really does at least occasionally happen). It is made of cast and machined aluminum to keep the saw lightweight, and the horizontal D handle gives a superb grip.

Compound Mitre Saws

Compound mitre saws come in two styles, with the least expensive being similar to chop mitre saws, in that the blade and motor unit pivots at the rear of the table. The second type has an additional pivot that allows a vertical plane tilt as well as the horizontal arc of the blade. These saws are as accurate as any power mitre saw, but have a somewhat limited cutting capacity: The 10-inch compound mitre saw with the largest cutting capacity seems to be the Ryobi TS-260, which will cut a 2 × 6 at 90 degrees, and has a maximum material width of $4\frac{3}{16}$ inches at 45 degrees. The TS-260 cuts to $3\frac{5}{16}$ inches deep, about $\frac{3}{16}$ inch short of cutting a full 4 × 4 post.

Mitre Saws

Proper use for any mitre saw is reasonably simple: Set your angles as accurately as possible and lock the table in place (this is usually done by twisting the handle to the right; twisting it to the left unlocks the table). Make sure that the workpiece is snugly in place against both the base of the machine and the fence.

Keep in mind the fact that all of these power mitre saws will fling material, and fling it hard. Once you've had a $\frac{1}{2}$ × 2-inch chunk of wood whistle by your face, you'll do your best to make sure it doesn't happen again, but it's best to prevent it from happening at all. Make sure the wood is securely held against the rear fence, clamped if possible. Do not place the arc of bowed wood towards the fence! If wood bows or arcs in any way, keep the inside of that bow arc facing you as you cut, to prevent binding—this cannot be overemphasized! Always make sure the saw blade stops before you lift it from the cut. My first experiences with power mitre saws were lessons in patience, because a couple of times I lifted the blade—let it spring back, really—without checking to see if I was finished cutting, only to find that the blade also lifted a small piece of wood, which then zinged by my head.

Always support the ends of long work pieces: Having work tilt up into a spinning blade can cause injury and a host of lesser problems, such as ruining the wood you've just cut to accurate size and angle.

Finally, and most important, keep your body and face out of line with the blade, so any cutoff flies by the target area instead of using you for a bull's-eye. Naturally, you should wear safety goggles, and make sure you have no jewelry, clothing, hair, etc., that might get caught in the blade. Also, keep your hands at least 4 inches from the blade at all times. I may be shown in the illustrations in this book not wearing goggles over my glasses. My glasses have specially reinforced lenses, although goggles would still serve as a good first line of defense.

Selecting Your Saw

Any woodworker who isn't going to do professional work

might consider a straight 10-inch mitre saw or one of the single-pivot 8¼-inch consumer models a reasonable purchase, if his intent is to continue only lightly with carpentry or woodworking. If you use larger mitre saws a lot, it might be worthwhile to buy one, but for occasional or intermittent use, check rental prices in your locality. For those of us who do extensive mitring, the justification for buying one of the saws that costs upwards of $300 is hard but can be found. You must consider your needs carefully, check a few of the tools to see which suits you best fiscally and physically, and then buy the one that most closely meets these requirements.

One of the more costly compound mitre saws may perform one job well and quickly that you will be doing with some frequency. If so, you should consider buying it. If not, or if you already have a good radial arm saw and don't require a portable saw, then a simple mitre saw is probably best. Skil, Porter Cable, Milwaukee, Ryobi, Sears, and Makita all sell good-quality simple mitre saws.

For large-capacity work, slide compound models are usually best, although DeWalt's 12-inch mitre saw does have a large cutoff capacity at any available angle, particularly when compared to any chop mitre saw.

Smaller, less expensive compound-mitre saws are available, and may suit you if you do very little angle cutting. They tend to wear quickly and go out of adjustment more easily than do the heavy-duty models. Otherwise, look for at least a 10-inch mitre saw or an 8½ or 10-inch slide compound-mitre saw at the pro level. They cost more (except for straight mitre saws in the 10-inch range), but are far more durable and accurate. And don't forget the hand mitre boxes.

Moulding and Bevel Cuts

For moulding and bevel cuts on birdhouses, consider the compound-mitre saws, which, of course, serve for the other angle cuts, too. Small compound-mitre saws do light work well, and the heavier-duty models described take just about anything you care to throw at them, within their rated capacities.

Mitre and compound-mitre saws are strong assets when building any project, and the more complex a project is, the more valuable these saws become in today's woodworking shop. Some experts, in fact, have recently replaced radial arm saws with compound-mitre saws, using the slide versions with capacities in the 12-inch (width of cut) range. I don't think such a saw will replace my Delta 12-inch radial arm saw, for several reasons: my Delta saw has a crosscut capacity of *over* 15 inches, well beyond the capacity of any compound-mitre saw on the market; and no compound mitre saw that I know of

makes wide dado cuts, which my radial arm saw does well because the cuts are visible as they're being made. Also, it is less dangerous to use a radial arm saw to cut grooves than to cut them with the overarm blade on the mitre saw.

Radial Arm Saws

For many birdhouse project jobs, a radial arm saw will be the most helpful tool. Its overarm construction provides an unobstructed view of the blade making cuts that is not possible with table saws. The saw also offers quick and easy cutoff capabilities, often up to more than 15 inches (the larger, more powerful, and more costly the saw, of course, the greater the rip and crosscut capabilities).

The radial arm saw, however, shouldn't be the single saw used in a shop that does not have another major wood-cutting saw. Radial arm saws are extremely limited in their crosscut and rip widths (although their rip width is usually a few inches greater than the crosscut width). That's the primary objection to the radial arm saw as *the* saw in a single-saw shop. There's another objection: The radial arm saw has a tendency towards extremely violent kickbacks during rip operations. Realistically, any saw with a circular blade traveling at the speed these blades travel is going to kick back, but the radial arm saw is even more likely to do so than the table saw—and the table saw is liable to at just about any time your attention relaxes. It has only been a year or so since I caught an 18-inch square chunk of ¾-inch-thick plywood in the chest while making a dado on a table saw. And it was my own fault for not paying enough attention and allowing my grip to relax.

Kickback is a fact of life in woodworking shops, but there are things you can do to minimize the chances of kickback when using a radial arm saw. Study the kickback lines, and use hold-downs and push sticks to help reduce it. Also, work with your body out of the kickback path. That's really the best protection for those times when both machinery safety items and your attention fail.

I love radial arm saws for the job they do making cutoffs, bevels and grooves on top of boards, along with general cutting work, although these days I almost never use a radial arm saw for ripping lumber. Also, some radial arm saws are equipped with accessory arbors to allow even greater flexibility with router bits, flexible shafts, and other tools. I know of no table saw or compound mitre saw that can be so equipped.

As a practical matter, the radial arm saws in a shop seem to get almost all the cutoff work for longer boards; this is because you have to construct a special table for the compound-mitre saw, while the radial arm saw comes with a table and usually a stand, and may already be set up so that it aligns with many other tables and bench tops of fairly standard height.

Radial arm saws come in a wide range of prices and capabilities. Lightweight saws, such as the Ryobi 8¼-inch model, make good crosscuts and bevel cuts, and are readily portable. Middle-range saws such as the various Sears Craftsman units are fairly portable, but are best used in a shop where they are not moved around; they are set up once and their accuracy is maintained when they aren't moved around. Big saws such as my Delta 12-inch saw may be listed as portable, but that's optimistic for a saw over 300 pounds. However, it is accurate and durable, has a good cutting depth, and is moderately priced.

Table and radial arm saws excel at certain jobs. The table saw is best at ripping, grooving, and similar jobs (and crosscutting when a sliding table is added). Radial arm saws are excellent at crosscutting (Illus. 5–18), dadoing, compound-cutting, and cutting dadoes or grooves on the visible side (upper side) of a piece of lumber, and may be fitted with many of the accessories (dado head, moulding head, etc.) that also fit table saws. Radial arm saws also may be fitted, depending on the brand of saw, with rotary shapers, flexible shafts, and router bits.

If you have to have one major saw in your shop, the table saw is best, but if at all possible, have both a table saw and a radial arm saw. Some experts prefer the radial

Illus. 5–18. The Delta 12-inch radial arm saw is a fairly heavy saw, but it can make wider and deeper cuts than one that is lightweight.

arm saw, but I like the slightly greater safety of the table saw during ripping operations, and its somewhat more durable setup. (Table saws tend to stay accurate when not moved, while radial arm saws, except for the absolutely top-grade models, will not remain accurate as long, and are less accurate at the end of setup.) Also, the radial arm saw is difficult to maintain.

A radial arm saw performs two tasks extremely well. First, you can cut very deep dadoes when they are needed (a 10-inch radial arm saw will operate an 8-inch dado set, while a 10-inch table saw will not run more than a 6-inch dado set). Second, when you use a dado or a moulding head, you can create some very fine multiple cuts and shapes because you are able to view the cuts. And it is easy to set up to make multiple dadoes, as you do when creating dentil moulding.

Do not attempt to rip-cut with a radial arm saw. Such work is better performed with a table saw, or, when you're desperate and not in a rush, with a band saw. I'll do ploughing and other ripping operations at less than full depth on the radial arm saw, but with extreme care, and on long pieces with a helper standing at the switch to cut it off if I yell.

I am curious about the Shopsmith 2000 saw, because it offers a feature no other saw does. It makes a 12-inch crosscut like a table saw, after which you can pull the *blade* through the work, as you do with the radial arm saw. The accuracy of any mitre cut is increased when the stock is held still and an accurately adjusted saw is pulled through it. That's one of the reasons for the success of power mitre saws and compound mitre saws.

Bench-top radial arm saws are available from Ryobi and Sears; these saws have a relatively small cutting capacity. Their blades are 8¼ inches in diameter, while the diameter of a standard blade is 10 inches. Obviously, this lessens the cutting depth by an inch. The motor speeds of these saws tend to be high (the no-load speed of the Ryobi is 5000 rpm), so there is some problem with the blade climbing through work as it is fed. You have to be conscious of this possibility and hold the power head back to the proper feed or the blade will climb and the motor stall. The newest version of the Ryobi bench-top radial arm saw has a climb-reduction feature.

These bench-top radial arm saws offer an 18,500 rpm speed accessory spindle (on the side of the motor opposite the arbor) for use with router bits. The high speed is an advantage here, because router bits are designed to work at speeds over 10,000 rpm and up to about 25,000 rpm.

Plate Joiners

Plate joiners (Illus. 5–19), also known as biscuit joiners,

Illus. 5–19. A Porter-Cable plate joiner has been used to cut these slots.

are the tool to use to joint wide boards when you don't want to use plywood. These tools allow you to glue up boards quickly and accurately with far greater ease than if you used dowels, and make joints far stronger than edge-to-edge butt joints. The biscuits or plates are flat, football-shaped, and all .148 inch thick no matter how wide they are. The saw blade on the tool cuts a kerf that is .156 inch thick, which allows the biscuit to fit loosely in the kerf. The plates absorb water from the glue and rapidly swell up to over .160 inch.

All of the models from European companies have a number of things in common, including one of the screwiest handle setups seen on any tool. They are also extremely noisy—all the machines from Europe *exceed* 100 decibels, a level that is rough on one's hearing.

The Porter-Cable 555 biscuit joiner has three advantages over the European joiners and other American joiners. It is by far the quietest portable unit on the market, because it is driven by a belt instead of helical gears. The belt drive also allows for a different shape, so the Porter-Cable 555 is also the easiest joiner to handle in general. It is also cheaper than other joiners because of the belt drive (belts and pulleys, even those made of the best material are far cheaper than gears).

Jointing Accuracy

Jointing accuracy is far easier to accomplish with plates than it is with dowels. The slot cut to accept the plate will allow adjustment along the length of the biscuit, while a dowel is restricted to one particular area. If you've drilled your dowel holes a fraction of an inch off, your project will be a fraction of an inch off. With plates, you'll never be much more than slightly off because of the way the joiners are made. If you are, adjust the biscuits until the parts mate perfectly.

There are some problems possible when using joiners. I left the first load of plates sent to me out in the open, in large plastic bins on my pegboard. There isn't a single usable biscuit left from this first load of 3,000 biscuits. My best suggestion for the average user is to buy biscuits just about as needed, to buy them in small packages, and to buy only a single package of each type. Do not open any of the packages until you need the biscuits, and reseal them as soon as possible. Store the packages in a dry place.

There seems no major difference between the generic brands of biscuit and the more costly brand names. It makes sense to get the cheapest available when the only difference is cost and name. Biscuits are made of solid beech and stamped to size after being sawn into laths.

Basic Joiner Technique

Biscuits are used to join surfaces; they replace splines or dowels for this process and usually do a neater, quicker job. Gluing is simple: First use a screwdriver or knife to remove chips from the slots and then dribble glue along the sides of the slots.

As with any joint preparation, the wood must be cut accurately, with the ends squared or mitred as needed for the junction to be made. The better the overall preparation, the better the resulting joint. The cuts are aligned using marks on the joiners. My Porter-Cable 555 joiner operates a little differently (especially with mitres) than the others because of its different handle and blade-drive system (Illus. 5–20).

The joiner has a mark that extends up the front of the baseplate. This is the center point of the work being cut with the plate joiner. Lining this mark up with one board, and then with a second board, ensures that those boards will line up easily when the cuts are made.

Many of the glue and nail joints in my birdhouses can be replaced with biscuits and glue, if you wish.

Edge-to-Edge Joining

Mark where you expect to need the plates to add strength to the joint. This will be at 8-inch or wider intervals for edge-to-edge joining.

Work with two boards at a time, no matter how many you're joining. Mark the boards 2 inches in from their ends, and about 8–10 inches apart between those marks.

Place the cutting guide so the slot is cut about halfway down the board's thickness. Cut the marks on both boards; then insert biscuits and check the joint. If necessary, clean out the grooves.

Disassemble the practice setup, apply the glue, insert the biscuits one last time, and clamp the boards together, in alignment. When the glue has set, repeat the process on the next pair of boards.

Final preparation of the resulting wide board is simple light sanding; it will take less time than sanding most other edge-to-edge glued joints.

Corner Joining

It is in joining corners that biscuit joinery really is helpful. Align the pieces, but this time the end of the top board should face you, sitting flush on top of the end of, and at right angles to, the bottom board. Make your marks 2 inches in from the ends and every 4 to 6 inches between the initial marks.

Cut the slots, starting with the face board. Then cut the slots in the end of the other board. If you use any joiner but the Porter-Cable 555, you will find yourself cutting into the end piece with little to brace the joiner. Line up some bracing material on which to rest the joining tool.

Next, test-fit the joint using dry plates. Then disassemble it, add glue, and reassemble it with clamps.

* * *

Illus. 5–20. The Porter-Cable 555 joiner set to cut slots for biscuits that will support the mitres.

6. Gluing and Clamping

When considering gluing procedures, your first concern should be whether the woods being glued will successfully mate. Great differences in moisture content in woods create problems. Differences in wood structure may also create problems (for example, teak, with its high silicone and oil contents, does not bond well with other woods; it is even difficult to bond teak to itself, and usually requires epoxy adhesives).

The best wide-area glue-ups (especially sizable laminates or glued-up flat boards) result when the same wood species is used. Simply put, this means the entire board is made of pine, fir, oak, cherry, etc. If part of the board is cherry and part is pine, there will be difficulties, although these can be reduced by checking the chart on pages 41 and 42. This chart is from the United States Forest Products Laboratory.

Plain-sawed boards are best used with plain-sawed boards, and quarter-sawed boards with quarter-sawed. Otherwise, the differences in grain directions create distortion problems over time.

You'll also find it best to allow boards to temper. If you are using different kinds of lumber, or the same kinds from different sources, allow all of the lumber to remain at least 24 hours in the environment in which it will be glued. This stabilizes the moisture content of the wood for the environment at hand, making for a more successful glue-up.

SELECTING A WOODWORKING GLUE

You'll note an array of so-called woodworking glues in many catalogs and ads. There are not as many true woodworking glues around as one might expect; even fewer are of true interest to the woodworker making birdhouses.

Woodworking adhesives can be categorized into animal glues and synthetics. Animal glues are older, and less used today because the synthetics offer properties that they do not. There are some properties offered by animal glues that synthetics do not offer, or do not offer as completely, but those are generally unimportant to the birdhouse builder. Animal glues are barely water-resistant, so are totally useless outdoors. Below I describe synthetic adhesives.

Synthetic Adhesives

Most woodworking adhesives used today are synthetics, formulated for various type applications in woodworking and other fields. Most are types of resin glue that gather strength by chemical reaction, or curing. Curing is dependent on the temperature of the glue line. The strength and speed of the cure may be increased by increasing the glue-line temperature (within certain limits, below 120 degrees Fahrenheit for all glues). New types are being added almost daily, and I'm currently awaiting a couple of samples for testing, such as Gorilla Glue (a polyurethane glue with a vinegar cleanup).

White Glues (Polyvinyl Resins)

White glues (polyvinyl resins) come in up to gallon and larger jugs ready to use in squeeze bottles. There are many manufacturers and brands of liquid white glues. These types of glue should not be of much interest to birdhouse makers, unless you're doing work that is to be solely decorative. They are somewhat more water-resistant than animal glues, but not enough to make a real difference outdoors.

White glues do not offer a chemical reaction cure. The water in the glue moves into the wood and into the air; thus, the resin gels. On unstressed joints, you can release clamping pressure in 45 minutes, but leaving clamping pressure on for several hours is better. Stressed joints must have at least a six-hour set before the clamps are released.

White glues are not always truly white—some are dyed close to yellow to appear more like aliphatic resin glues (liquid yellow glues). Aliphatic-resin glues are more heat- and water-resistant.

Liquid Yellow Glues (Aliphatic resin)

Aliphatic resin glues are improvements over the polyvinyl-resin glues. Their heat resistance is a good deal higher, which greatly improves their sandability, as well as their strength at temperatures of 100 degrees Fahrenheit or higher. These glues set well at temperatures of up to 110 degrees, which means they can be used in some of the hottest summer weather possible. Raising the glue-line temperature speeds the set rate, reducing the open assembly time.

Yellow glues are less likely to run and drip than white glues because their basic consistency is heavier. This makes for neater gluing jobs, and their greater moisture resistance means projects may be worked on in damp areas. Under no circumstances, though, is yellow glue to be used outdoors. Yellow glue is suitable on interior birdhouse projects used for decoration, or on those projects where paint or another finish is carefully applied over all glue lines.

Yellow glues set faster than white glues, which is a problem for complex projects. Complex birdhouses should be glued up in stages of assembly. Yellow glue completely cures in 24 hours, its glue line is a translucent pale tan or amber color; and water cleanup (before set) is possible (Illus. 6–1).

Waterproof Glues

Waterproof glues are the most useful glues for the birdhouse maker. There are a number of them available for use with wood, but the two most traditional ones are urea-resin (also known as plastic-resin) and resorcinol-resin glues.

Resorcinol-resin glues are dark red liquids (the resins) to which a catalytic powder is added before use. Plastic-resin glues are highly water-resistant, but only resorcinol glues are waterproof. Where possible, use plastic-resins glues because resorcinol resin glues cost at least three times, sometimes four times, more. Each is described below more thoroughly.

Resorcinol-resin glues have a fair working life, after mixing, that ranges from about 15 to 120 minutes. It is best to go with glues that have a longer working life, so check the label. Brush the resorcinol on, or spread it with a spatula (tongue depressors, available at any drugstore, make great glue spreaders, as do ice cream sticks and toothpicks for small projects). Immediately tighten the glued surface with a heavy clamp.

Before starting to bond anything with resorcinol, make sure the moisture content of the wood is below about 12 percent, the joints are tight and fit precisely, and heavy-duty clamps are ready. Use a high clamping pressure, about 200 pounds per square inch (p.s.i.). The glue line is ugly, a dark red or reddish-brown color.

TiteBond II

TiteBond II was the first in the line of "weatherproof" adhesives (Illus. 6–1). It is not totally waterproof to the extent that it can be used for boatbuilding, but it is water-resistant enough so that it can be used on birdhouse projects.

This glue has qualities similar to aliphatic-resin adhesives, and costs about $2.00 a gallon more, not much considering how many birdhouses you can glue up with a gallon of glue.

Urea-Resin Glues

Urea (or plastic) resin glues are dry powders, mixed with water just before use. The urea formaldehyde resin pro-

Illus. 6–1. For outdoor use, and especially in glue/nail work, TiteBond II wood glue has always served me well.

vides a highly water-resistant adhesive, best used on wood with a moisture content of no more than 12 percent. It is best used—and cures—at a temperature of 70 degrees Fahrenheit. This glue is hard to beat for birdhouse use: It is waterproof for all intents and purposes, low in cost, and easy to use.

Urea-resin glues are superb for producing joints in projects that have to withstand long-term dampness. Some do well in true exterior applications. They make good general-purpose glues because they work easily in all situations (with the exception of high-density woods such as maple and oak). Precise fit of joints is essential, because urea-resin glues are not good gap fillers (the best gap filler, other than epoxies, is animal or hide glue).

Setting of the glue is affected by temperature, so complex assembly jobs must be glued up when the temperature is cool. The glue's working life ranges from one to five hours. The clamp pressure should be moderate, and the clamps should be in place for at least nine hours. Check that the squeezed-out glue is cured hard before removing the clamps.

The glue line is an attractive light tan color, and gumming is not a problem because the adhesive resists heat well.

Epoxy Adhesives

Like resorcinols, epoxies are two-part adhesives in which a liquid hardener is added to a liquid resin. Curing is by a chemical reaction, with heat given off as the reaction takes place.

Mix only small quantities of epoxies. They are easier to work with that way, and waste is costly.

Epoxies can be formulated to suit just about any bonding need anyone can come up with in moderate temperature applications, so it is essential to follow package directions precisely when using any brand. Make sure you *need* an epoxy's features before using any but the smallest amount. This is the most expensive of all wood glues.

Epoxy doesn't shrink at all, so is a good gap filler. Some epoxies are available as putties; these can fill even the largest gaps, although you should fit joints precisely to ensure a long project life.

It is not financially practical to use epoxies for general woodworking jobs such as bonding strips of wood to form a butcher block or bonding wood for a tabletop, but they're ideal for spot-gluing of decorative items for exterior use and for adding decorations to birdhouses (cupolas, spires, etc.).

Epoxies are very toxic, too, which limits their use in some shops. And they are also messy; you can avoid getting them on your hands by wearing thin plastic gloves, now available in packs of 100. Any mess can be cleaned up quickly with acetone (fingernail polish remover). When using it, keep the gloves on, and make sure all mixing containers and sticks are disposed of. When you have to fill gaps for any reason, epoxies will be well worth using, despite the problems just cited. Epoxies require light clamping pressure and their working time is adjustable (depending on the system, it can be as great as 90 minutes). Their gap-filling capacity and strength are incredible, and the resulting glue line is either clear or an amber color (depending on the brand used). Some kinds of epoxies do not stain wood, while others do. Fillers can be used as can pigments.

Hot-Melt Adhesives

Hot-melt adhesives are available to home-shop workers in stick and sheet forms, often with the sheet forms supplied as the backing to edging of different kinds. I do a fair amount of work with oak plywood, so oak edging in 250-foot rolls, with the adhesive already in place, makes sense. This joins easily with an electric flat iron.

Hot-melt adhesive hold materials for pad cutting without nail holes. It works well at holding small items in place for routing, too, and is easily peeled off later. Depending on the formulation, hot melts set from about two to 30 seconds. Their best use is for temporary joints, because the overall joint strength, regardless of manufacturers' claims, is far lower than that normally required of good woodworking joints.

Hot-melt glue does not sand well at all. It gums up in a hurry, as friction from the sandpaper creates heat. Slice off any residue for easy cleanup.

Hand pressure is all that is required to get a bond, but you'll find things work a lot better if you're in a shop that has a temperature upwards of 85 degrees Fahrenheit. This warms the wood so the hot glue doesn't set too rapidly and create a poor bond.

Selection Guidelines

The selection of the appropriate glue is important, but the application of the glue and the clamping of the parts is just as important.

For general uses, liquid yellow glues and polyvinyl acetate (white resin) glues work fine; use white glue for longer assembly times, and yellow glue for better moisture resistance, better sanding, and better gap filling.

For water resistance, select either epoxy or urea resin; if possible, select urea resin, unless epoxies fill some other need, such as gap filling, etc. Epoxies cost too much to be general-use glues.

For waterproofing, use resorcinol resins. They are expensive, difficult to apply properly (requiring very precise fitting joints), and ugly, but impervious to water.

Because you want to make birdhouses almost exclusively with water-resistant or waterproof glues, the following information concerns only these two types of glue. Remember, however, yellow glues may be water-resistant enough to allow you to put two or three coats of paint or other finish over the glue lines and leave the project outdoors.

Most adhesives can be applied with brush, stick, or roller. Clean off any dust, oil, old glue, loosened and torn-up grain, and chips. A test assembly is a good idea, because once the glue is added, correcting mistakes is messy. If the glue sets, mistakes remain.

Mix all adhesives according to the maker's directions, and as accurately as possible. Spread them over the surfaces to be joined.

CLAMPS

Clamping pressure on a glue joint does three jobs. Wood surfaces must be brought into close contact with the glue, the glue must become a smooth, thin, continuous

Gluing and Clamping

film, and the joint must also be held steady after those jobs are carried out.

Clamping pressure varies with glue type, but basically the heavier the glue, the more clamping pressure needed. Go for a thin, smooth glue line, not a joint that is squeezed dry from too much pressure.

Most woodworking glues on softwoods fall in the middle-thickness range, taking clamp pressure of 100 to 150 p.s.i. (pounds per square inch). Dense hardwoods may require pressures of up to 300 p.s.i. Resorcinol and urea resins require a great deal of pressure, while epoxy requires very little.

To determine the pounds per square inch being applied, divide the pressure exerted by the clamp by the size of the project. Home-shop workers may occasionally apply too much pressure using hand-tightened clamps, but this is unlikely. Any time the work starts to bow, lighten the pressure, and you should face no problems.

Avoid excessive pressure in favor of even pressure over an entire assembly. It is better to even glue squeeze-out over the entire unit than to apply pressure that is too tight.

Use clamps every 8 to 10 inches when possible, spacing some light types every 4 to 6 inches. In no case should you space clamps out more than 16 inches.

Types of Clamps

Woodworking clamps fall into four categories: bar clamps, hand screws, C-clamps, and band clamps. Pipe clamps, picture-frame clamps, mitre clamps, and other types fall into each of these categories. The largest number of different clamps fall in the bar clamp category.

The size of *bar clamps* varies with the weight of the clamp. The heavier the clamp, the longer it is, so normal-weight clamps are about 48 inches long, while light-duty clamps reach a maximum length of 32 inches. Very light-duty notched cam-and-tongue bar clamps have a maximum length of 24 inches. Heavy-duty clamps reach lengths of 98 inches. These expensive, smooth-working clamps are superb for heavy work, but are not much help with birdhouses.

Short, lightweight bar clamps are a help in some areas where *C-clamps* are used, such as with two glued-up sheets of plywood, etc. It takes just as many bar as C-clamps, but the former have more depth of throat and can clamp somewhat thicker material.

Band clamps vary in size. Stanley Tools clamps are about 1 inch wide and 10 feet long, and Vermont-American clamps are 2 inches wide and 14 feet long. Both are excellent tools. Band clamps are used to clamp odd shapes, whether these be octagon frames, chair-leg assemblies, or picture frames.

Hand screws are great for clamping when you do not want to mar the wood. They work well for clamping non-parallel surfaces, and do not creep.

Hand-screw bodies are made of wood and are thus susceptible to all problems associated with a messy gluing job. To keep glue buildup from becoming a problem, coat the entire outer jaw with paste wax (don't polish it off). However, over the years, the wax will create enough slickness to make using the hand-screw tips quite difficult—small objects tend to slide out. Therefore, a better option is to cover the front of the hand screws, where the glue is most likely to get spread, with 2- or 3-inch-wide masking tape. Strip it off when it becomes loaded, and replace it.

GLUING PROPERTIES OF DIFFERENT SPECIES OF WOOD

Group One

This group glues very easily with glues that have a wide range of properties and under a wide range of gluing conditions.

Group One Hardwoods
Aspen
Chestnut
American Cottonwood
Black Willow
Yellow Poplar

Group One Softwoods
Bald Cypress
White Fir
Grand Fir
Noble Fir
Pacific Silver Fir
California Red Fir
Western Larch

Group Two

This group glues well with glues that have a fairly wide range of properties under a moderately wide range of gluing conditions.

Group Two Hardwoods
Red Alder
Basswood
Butternut
American Elm
Rock Elm

Hackberry
Magnolia
Mahogany
Sweetgum

Group Two Softwoods
Douglas Fir
Western Hemlock
Eastern White Pine
Southern Pine
Ponderosa Pine
Eastern Red Cedar
Western Red Cedar
Redwood
Sitka Spruce

Group Three

This group glues satisfactorily with good-quality glue under well-controlled gluing conditions.

Group Three Hardwoods
White Ash
Black Cherry
Dogwood
Soft Maple

Red Oak
White Oak
Pecan
Sycamore
Black Tupelo
Water Tupelo
Black Walnut

Group Three Softwoods
Alaska Cedar

Group Four

This group requires very close control of glue and gluing conditions, or special treatment, to obtain the best results.

Group Four Hardwoods
American Beech
Sweet Beech
Yellow Beech
Hickory
Hard Maple
Osage Orange
Persimmon

*   *   *

7. Birdhouse Plans

In this chapter you'll find designs for birdhouses that range in size from those for very small birds to those that either will fit, or can be adjusted to fit, very large birds. Some of these houses are more easily adjustable in size than are others. If it's a simple matter of raising a roof or lengthening a wall, as it is for many of them, the house can be used for any size bird, with just a few parts changed. If many other changes are needed, try to find another of the plans that will suit your purposes with less work. There are over 30 birdhouse plans, so one will suit your needs.

One note of caution: *Never* cut out multiple pieces of any plan without first making a sample of that project, whether it be a tiny birdhouse or huge dresser. Most projects indicate that you should measure the assembly while building the parts, to determine the actual sizes of the last few parts in the assembly. This is done to help you save time and money in case the dimensions for one of the parts happens to be off.

A number of the plans are whimsical. If whimsy doesn't strike your fancy, go with the more sedate styles. The birds don't care which you use, nor do they care much about which materials you use, although the floor size, house height, and entry-hole size are all important to them.

USING DIFFERENT MATERIALS

Wherever plywood is specified, you can also use either oriented strand board (OSB) or wafer board, to save on costs. It is, in fact, usual to use OSB or wafer board when the material will be covered by another material. If OSB or wafer board is used as an exterior material, it must receive a coat or two of exterior finish of some kind before exposure to the weather. The wood itself will change dimensions if not protected.

I often use pressure-treated wood for roofs, steeples, fences, and other parts that are not in constant contact with skin or feathers of nesting birds, so that they need little care over time. If pressure-treated wood is used for floors and walls, it should receive at least two coats of paint (enamel) or clear finish initially, and an additional two coats every six months or every year. Pressure treating is a means of conserving the scrap and occasional furniture-grade wood that is used on birdhouses.

GOURD BIRDHOUSE

It's hard to get any simpler than with a plain, old-fashioned gourd. For the basic gourd birdhouse, all you really need are a dried gourd, a pocketknife, and some wire or string. The version described and illustrated here (Illus. 7–1) is slightly fancier.

Tools

Drill
1⅛″ Forstner drill bit
2″-wide masking tape
3⁄32″ drill bit
Paint brush

Materials

One large, dried gourd
2″ square of duct tape
Exterior polyurethane

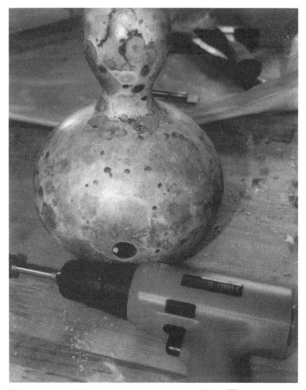

Illus. 7–1. The gourd birdhouse. Use Forstner drill bits carefully when drilling the entry hole.

Instructions

Start by drilling through the top of the gourd where the stem joins—if you drill into the stem, so much the better.

Next, lay on at least one coat of exterior polyurethane and allow six hours for drying. Tape over the area in which you wish to drill your hole. Before drilling, use an awl to make a centering hole for the bit, to keep the bit from "walking." Be careful when drilling or hammering the gourd; gourds are fairly sturdy, but not as sturdy as wood.

With the hole drilled, hang the gourd from a high spot in the shop and add at least two more coats of exterior polyurethane. Before the last coat, place the duct tape over the hole in the bottom where the person who dried the gourd removed the seeds (if they weren't removed, you will find no hole and can shake the seeds out of the entry hole).

Voilà! Except for the drying time for the finish, this birdhouse takes about 15 minutes to construct. The polyurethane finish will help it last several years longer than a natural, no-finish look will.

Weatherproof wood glue
White enamel for base
Letters for sign

Tools

Claw hammer (10 or 13 ounces)
Pneumatic finish nailer or brad nailer
Mitre box
Handsaw
Square-shank screwdriver, or driver bit
Drill
1½″ Forstner bit
⅜″ bit
⅛″ bit for screw pilot holes
Laundry marker (to draw windows)
Square
Measuring tape
Awl
Finish sander (also known as pad sander)
Sandpaper (100 and 120 grit)
Paintbrush

FALSE-FRONT HOTEL

This redwood false-fronted hotel (Illus. 7–2 and 7–3) is suitable for western or eastern bluebirds, and offers a whimsical look at western America. There's even a porch that offers shade and protects the parents while they are feeding their babies. Assembly is straightforward, with only a few angles needing cutting.

Materials

One piece of ¾ × 10 × 12″ plywood, for the *base*
One piece of 1 × 9 × 9¼″ redwood, for the *roof*
One piece of 1 × 8¼ × 9¼″ redwood, for the *front*
One piece of 1 × 3½ × 8¼″ redwood, for the *porch roof*
One piece of 1 × 6¾ × 4¼″ redwood, for the *back*
Two pieces of 6⅜ (4⅜″ at rear) × 7⅜ × 1″ redwood, for the *sides*
Two ⅜″ diameter × 8″ long dowels
Two #8 × 1¼″ square-drive screws with super-round washer heads, to hold roof on
¼ lb. #4 nails or pneumatic nailer and brads

Instructions

Start by cutting all pieces to size. Next, cut a 15-degree bevel on the top of the back piece and the front of the

Illus. 7–2. This false-front Western hotel is a bit whimsical, but eventually weathers to an attractive, natural-looking grey color that birds like.

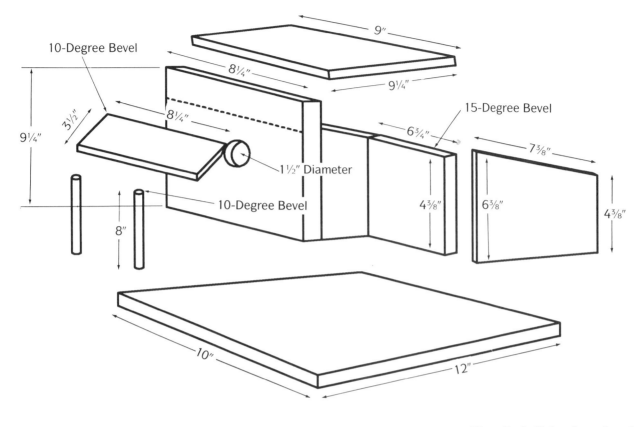

Illus. 7–3. False-front hotel.

roof; use a compound mitre saw, jointer, table saw, or other tool. You can use a plane for the bevelling if you wish to use only hand tools. The wood material used here is all redwood, except for the plywood base and birch dowels, so bevelling is easy. Reseat and bevel the back edge of the porch roof to 10 degrees.

Cut the sides with a mitre saw or mark one edge at 6⅜ inches and the other at 4⅜ inches and cut along the line that provides. Then place one side in a vise with its 6⅜-inch side up. Check its fit with the front, and then apply glue. Next, nail through the front onto the side, keeping the bottoms of the two pieces even; the upper part of the front extends over the front of the slanted edge of the side almost 3 inches. Nail the pieces together and remove them from the vise. Apply glue to the long edge of the second side, and position the piece on the assembly so that it is also correctly located. Nail it. Test-fit, glue, and nail the back in place.

Next, mark a line 7¼ inches up the exterior of the front, and scribe it across the part. Mark and scribe a 7-inch line on the interior part. Align the porch roof with the exterior line; check its fit, by making sure it aligns with the line above the roof's top back edge. Remove the

front, apply glue, and nail through its back into the porch roof, using the 7-inch-high line as a guide.

Sand the whole project lightly with 100- and 120-grit sandpaper. Then install the roof using two square-drive screws.

Next, center the assembled house on its base. First, apply glue, and then use 2-inch-wide masking tape to hold the house in its marked place. Then invert it. Make marks on the underside to provide nailing lines, and nail the base in place (Illus. 7–4).

Before nailing on the base, mark a line for your hotel lettering and add the lettering. Use vinyl stick-on letters, angularly arranged. Use a combination square to lay out and draw the windows; use a pencil and the square to lay out the shapes, and a laundry marker and the square to draw them.

With the birdhouse still inverted, calculate the distance you need to center holes for ⅜-inch dowels located 1 inch in from the outside edges of the birdhouse and 1½ inches out from the front wall. Drill the holes from the underside of the base all the way through the base. Bevel one end of each dowel at 10 degrees to match the underside of the roof. Insert the dowels through the holes, and

Illus. 7–4. The assembled hotel; the lettering and windows are in place, but the bottom is not yet nailed in.

Illus. 7–5. After bevelling the ends of the dowels to match the underside of the roof and drilling holes in the base, insert the dowels in the holes and mark them to cut off excess.

check their fit. Mark and cut off any excess dowel from the underside of the base. Place a touch of TiteBond II adhesive on the bevelled tip of each dowel after it is through the hole, and coat the last ½ inch or so with the glue. Glue securely holds the porch supports in place (Illus. 7–5).

This house installs easily. Just drive a screw down through the floor into the top of a post, and then reinstall the roof.

THREE BLUEBIRD HOUSES

These quick and easy projects (Illus. 7-6–7-9) can be built in minutes. The designs are similar to one used by various birding associations, but are my own adaptations. My bluebird houses are made of redwood, but cedar is also a fine wood for this project. Pine, poplar, and similar woods can also be used, but should be painted to endure the outdoors.

Materials

One piece of ¾ × 6 × 16″ redwood, for *back*
Two pieces of ¾ × 6 × 10½″ redwood, angled to 9½″ from back to front, for *sides*
Two pieces of ¾ × 6 × 9½″ redwood (bevelled 10 degrees at top), for *front and lid*
¾ × 4½ × 6″ redwood, for *floor*
One ¼″ #20 brass screw insert
One ¼ × 1½″ #20 brass thumbscrew

Birdhouse Plans

One Stanley CD5303 solid-brass hinge (2 × 1¾")
1 lb. 6d galvanized finishing nails

Tools

Combination square
Measuring tape
Saw (a circular or table saw is far faster than a
    handsaw)
Drill
1½", ¼", and ⅜" drill bits
Drill to fit screw insert (probably ⁷⁄₁₆", but check your
    screw insert first)
Claw hammer (13 or 16 ounces)
Nail set
Awl
Finish (pad) sander
Sandpaper (100 and 120 grit)

Instructions

First Version (Illus. 7-6–7-9)

Start by cutting the pieces, and then check all of them for
square. Assemble the box, attaching the sides to the
front and back with 6d galvanized nails. Install the sides
about 2½ inches down from the top of the back (the
overside back provides an area for you with which to

Illus. 7–6. I've placed many of these bluebird
birdhouses around my yard, and have found only
my choice of location might keep the birds away.

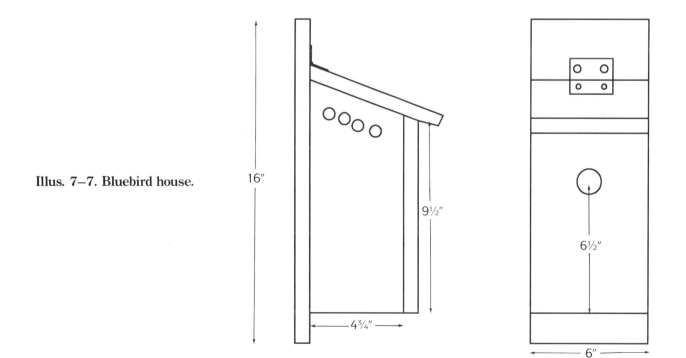

Illus. 7–7. Bluebird house.

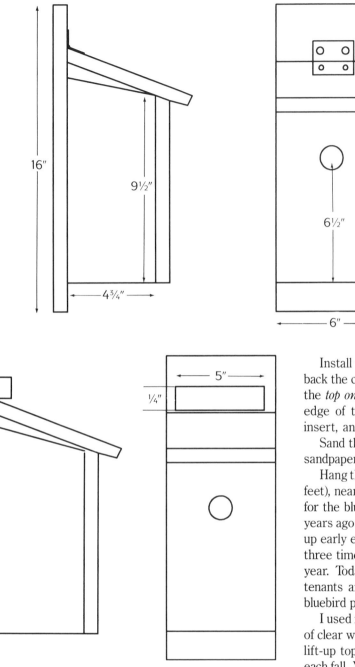

Illus. 7—8. Second version of the bluebird house.

Dimensions Identical to #1, Except for Cleat

Illus. 7—9. Third version of the bluebird house.

Install the top, centering the single hinge. Then mark back the correct distance and drill a ¼-inch hole through the *top only*. Mark the middle of that hole in the upper edge of the front. Drill the hole to accept the screw insert, and check the fit of the thumbscrew.

Sand the whole project lightly with 100- and 120-grit sandpaper.

Hang the birdhouse about chest high (approximately 4 feet), near (but not in) a brushy area or low tree, and wait for the bluebirds to arrive. I made several of these six years ago and hung them near my house. Only one went up early enough to draw a family, but we eventually had three times as many bluebirds as we had the preceding year. Today, one is still unoccupied, but the rest have tenants annually, further increasing the area's eastern bluebird population.

I used no finish on any of these birdhouses, but a coat of clear water repellent may add some years of use. The lift-up top allows you to easily clean out the birdhouse each fall. You can readily replace the knurled brass screw with a square-drive round washer screw, but remember to carry a driver for that when you're cleaning the houses.

Second Version (Illus. 7—8)

The second version varies only in that a short board (1¼ × ¾ × 5-inch redwood) is used instead of a hinge. Place the board on top of the birdhouse, and nail it to hold it firmly, without jamming. You can further simplify the

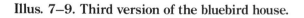

screw or nail the nesting box to a fence post, etc.). Install the floor next, using the same type of nails. Drill a ⅜-inch hole in each corner of the floor once it is nailed in place. This provides drainage. Drill at least three ⅜-inch holes near the top of each side, for ventilation.

construction by removing the brass screw-in thread and thumbscrew. To do this, use epoxy adhesive to glue on two ¾ × ½ × 4-inch redwood cleats spaced on the front bottom side of the lid so as to grip the front of the box firmly.

Third Version (Illus. 7—9)

The third version differs from the first one in that it has a differently tapered side that requires no ventilation-hole drilling. Cut the side square; that is, make its front and back the same height. This is different from the sides on the first version, which were 9½ inches long at the front and 10½ inches long at the back. The top is set at the same height (10½ inches), leaving a tapering 1-inch back-to-front gap, for ventilation. This removes one drilling step from the construction, making the birdhouse even simpler to build.

WREN HOUSE

My wren house (Illus. 7–10) differs from the bluebird houses primarily in side and roof design and in entry-hole size.

Materials

One piece of ¾ × 6 × 14″ redwood, for *backer board*
Two pieces of ¾ × 6 × 9½″ redwood, for *sides*. (The top side tapers from 9″ at front to 9½″ at back.)
Two pieces of ¾ × 6 × 9½″ redwood (bevelled 10° at top), for *front and lid*
One piece of ¾ × 4½ × 4″ redwood, for *floor*
One Stanley CD5303 solid-brass hinge (2 × 1¾″)
1 lb. 6d galvanized finished nails

Tools

Combination square
Measuring tape
Circular saw, table saw, or handsaw
Mitre saw or band saw and taper jig
1″ drill bit, for entry hole (use a 1⅛″ drill bit for Carolina wrens)
Drill
¼″ drill bit
Drill to fit screw insert (⁷⁄₁₆″, but check before drilling)
Claw hammer (13 or 16 ounces)
Nail set
Awl
Finish sander
Sandpaper (100 and 120 grit)

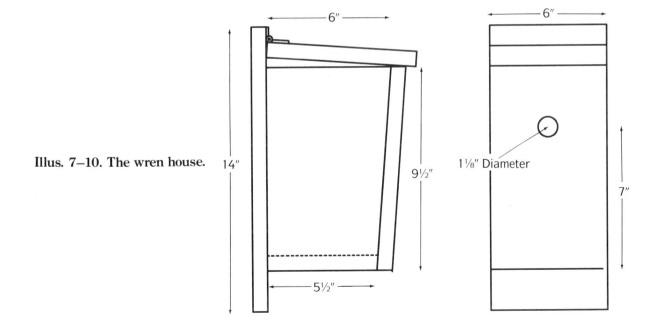

Illus. 7—10. The wren house.

Instructions

Cut the boards to their rough sizes, and then set the table-saw rip fence so that the taper jig will cut off ½ inch at one end of the 8½-inch boards, and nothing at the other end. Cut a single side taper on each of the side boards.

Next, nail the untapered sides of the side boards to the backer board, 2 inches down from its top. Then nail the front onto the tapered sides of the boards.

Check the fit of the bottom, or floor, and do *not* add a front taper. There should be a ¼-inch gap at the front of the floor where it doesn't quite meet the front of the nesting box. This allows for drainage. Sand the whole project lightly with 100- and 120-grit sandpaper. Place the top, or lid, on the birdhouse and adjust it to accept a hinge. Install the hinge and make two ¾ × 1 × 4″ cleats; nail and glue (with epoxy) the cleats to the underside of the top front, where they grip the front to prevent inadvertent opening of the nesting box, while allowing for easy cleaning.

All nesting boxes must be cleaned once a year. Doing the job in winter prevents you from coming in contact with wasps, which also use the nesting boxes.

DECORATED BIRDHOUSE

This simple unit (Illus. 7–11) can be made of redwood or pine and uses decorative doors and windows from Paul Meisel's Specialty Store in Mound, Minnesota, to add a unique quality. It has a standard eaved roof and a pivoting floor.

Materials

Two pieces of 1 × 6 × 6″ redwood, for the *sides*
Two pieces of 1 × 8 × 10″ redwood, for the *front and back*
Two pieces of 1 × 8 × 8″ redwood, for the *roof*
One piece of 1 × 6 × 5½″ redwood, for the *floor*
1 lb. 6d galvanized nails
Two 8d galvanized finishing nails
One 1½″ knurled-handle brass machine screw
One $^{10}\!/_{32}$ × ½″ brass-screw insert
White exterior paint
Asphalt roofing shingles
Two plastic windows

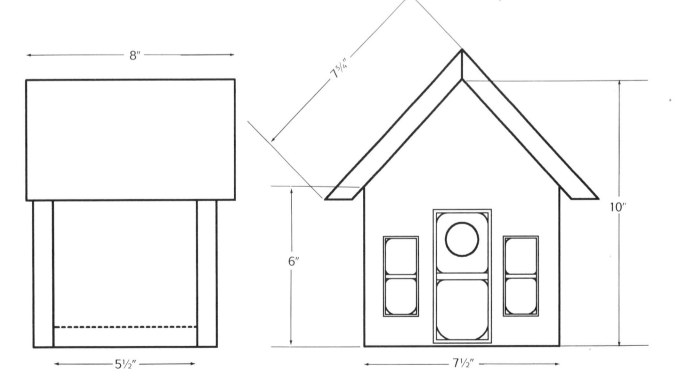

Illus. 7–11. Decorated birdhouse.

One plastic door
Dark blue spray paint

Tools

Handsaw (8 or 10 tooth)
Mitre box or power mitre box
Square
Measuring tape
Hammer
Screwdriver
Drill
Drill bit for knurled-handle brass machine screw
Drill bit for brass-screw insert
1″ or larger drill bit, for entry hole
Nail set
Awl
Finish (pad) sander
Sandpaper (100 and 120 grit)
Waterproof glue
2″-wide paintbrush

Instructions

Start by cutting all the pieces to size. Cut a 45-degree mitre on the front and back, to allow for a roof with a centered peak. Then assemble the sides inside the front and back, and install the roof along the eave lines.

Next, insert the floor for a test fit, and drill the hole for the knurled-handle screw into the lower edge of one side off center. Mark the middle of the screw insert through this hole. Then remove the floor and drill for the screw insert. Install the insert. Replace the floor and use two 8d galvanized nails as center pivots for the floor. Before placing the knurled screw, paint the entire assembly (except the roof top) white. Spray-paint one side of the doors and windows dark blue.

Next, install the asphalt shingles with waterproof glue. Then, after scraping off a bit of paint under where the doors and windows are located (so the epoxy will adhere better), glue the doors and windows in place, using epoxy glue.

Next, drill the 1½″ entry hole inside the upper door opening. If you wish to attract birds other than bluebirds, drill the hole a bit smaller (1 inch for nuthatches, 1⅛ inches for chickadees, 1¼ inches for titmice). Then sand the whole project lightly with 100- and 120-grit sandpaper.

Finally, install the knurled screw so that floor will *not*

pivot. When the handle on the screw is turned, the screw may be pulled out, and the floor pivoted around its 8d nails for cleaning.

NESTING BOX

This nesting box (Illus. 7–12), based on a time-tested design, is easy to construct and will last a long time if made of either cedar or redwood.

Materials

One piece of 1 × 10 × 6¼″ redwood or cedar, for the *front*
Two pieces of 1 × 6 × 7″ redwood or cedar, for the *sides*
One piece of 1 × 14¼ × 6″ redwood or cedar, for the *back*
One piece of 1 × 7 × 7¼″ redwood or cedar, for the *roof*
One piece of 1 × 3⅞ × 4″ redwood or cedar, for the *bottom*. (Cut a 45° bevel off ½ inch of at least two corners.)
¼ lb. 6d galvanized finishing nails
Six–eight 4d galvanized finishing nails
Four 3″ #7 square-drive screws, to fasten unit to fence post, pole, etc.

Tools

Circular saw
Drill
1½″ Forstner bit
Nail spinner
Hammer
Nail set
Measuring tape
Square
Screwdriver bit for drill

Instructions

Start by cutting all pieces to the sizes as indicated above. Mitre the sides 10 degrees from front to rear, and mitre the front 10 degrees from its top to bottom. Align the sides about 2 inches up on the back. The roof will then taper down, and will provide good ventilation.

Drill the 1¼-inch entry hole for wrens about 1 inch down from the top edge, and centered. Use a 1½-inch hole for bluebirds.

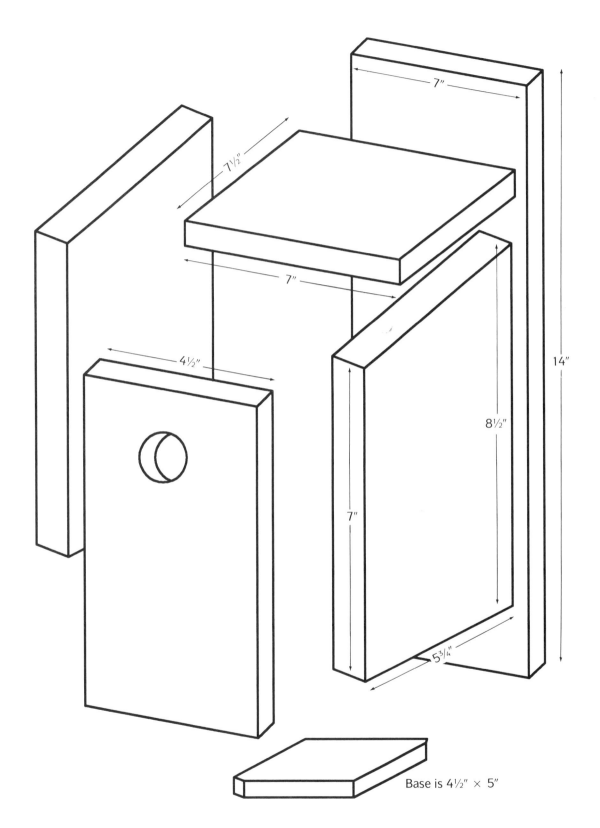

Illus. 7–12. Nesting box for wrens, bluebirds, and many other birds.

Birdhouse Plans

Next, set the back on the sides and nail and glue through the back into the sides using four nails per side. Then turn over the assembly and nail the front into the sides, using two or three nails and glue per side.

Lay the unit on one side and nail the bottom into the sides, one screw per side. The bottom may be installed with 8d finishing nails that are set the same distance from the back on each side, with a pullout, galvanized 10d common nail at the front to allow the bottom to spin and drop old nests, etc. In such cases, you may go ahead and nail the top on securely.

For a removable top, place the top on the assembly and mark the line along the front of the back board for the screws. Use two screws to hold the top in place. The nesting box is now assembled.

You may finish the nesting box, but this is not usually done. Usually, the wood is allowed to weather to a grey color over time. If you used pine, or something other than cedar or redwood, paint the nesting box, or coat it with clear *exterior* polyurethane.

Install the nesting box so that the bottom of the box is at least three feet from the ground, and about 10–20 feet from brush.

BLUEBIRD OR WREN BIRDHOUSE

Bluebirds and wrens are very popular birds, thus the reason for so many birdhouses designed exclusively for them. These birdhouses (Illus. 7–13 and 7–14) often fit nuthatches, titmice, and other birds with minor or no variations. Titmice like a 1¼-inch entry hole and a 4 × 4″ floor space, but seldom fly with a tape measure. If house sparrows, nuthatches, chickadees, and other birds use this house, you'll have to vary the size of the hole. Make the hole 1 inch in diameter for the brown-headed nuthatch, 1⅛ inches for chickadees, and 1½ inches for bluebirds, warblers, and tree swallows.

Materials

One piece of 1 × 6 × 14¼″ cedar, for the *back*
Two pieces of 1 × 7 × 5½″ cedar, for the *sides*
One piece of 1 × 7¼ × 7″ cedar, for the *roof*
One piece of 1 × 6 × 6¼″ cedar, for the *front*
One piece of 1 × 4⅜ × 4⅜″ cedar, for the *floor*
One ⅜ × 3″ dowel, for the perch
Two #8 × 1¼″ square-drive screws with super-round washer heads
#4 galvanized finishing nails
Weatherproof wood glue

Tools

Claw hammer (10 or 13 ounces)
Pneumatic finish nailer or brad nailer
Mitre box
Saw
Square-shank screwdriver, or driver bit
Drill
1¼″ Forstner bit
⅜″ drill bit
⅛″ bit for screw pilot holes
Square
Measuring tape
Awl
Finish sander
Sandpaper (100 and 120 grit)
Paintbrush

Instructions

Cut all pieces to size, and then use the mitre box to mitre the sides the required 10 degrees. Bevel the back of the roof at 10 degrees, too. Assemble the sides to the back with glue and nails; set the bottoms of the sides about 3½ inches up from the bottom edge of the back. Drill the proper-diameter entry hole and the hole for the perch dowel in the front. Place the front across the sides and nail and glue it securely.

Illus. 7–13. Bluebird or wren birdhouse, in cedar.

Mitres on Sides Are Both Ten degrees.

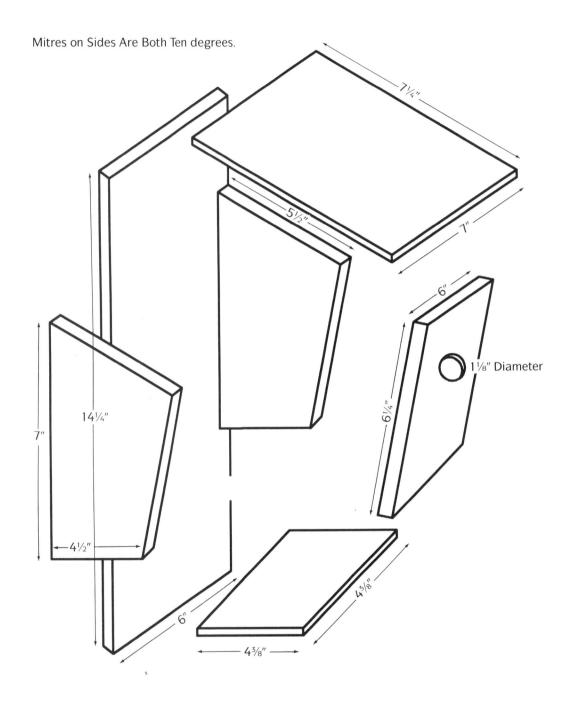

Illus. 7–14. Bluebird or wren birdhouse.

Next, place the roof on the assembly so it overlaps it evenly on both sides, and nail and glue it in place. Then check the fit of the bottom, making sure it's a bit loose (clip the back edges 45 degrees ½ inch in, to aid drain-age). Insert the bottom, drill pilot holes, and drive in screws to hold it in place.

Sand the entire assembly with 100- or 120-grit sand-paper and you're ready to hang the birdhouse.

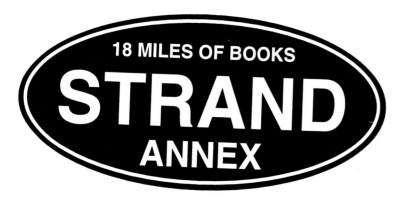
struction of this birdhouse isn't difficult. g all dowels to size and assembling the jig nts an L shape, with the upright leg ¾ inch wels to rest in during drilling (Illus. 7–18 the dowels in a standard mitre box. Power nd to chew up dowels and spit out pieces, re better with these thicker dowels than nes. It's safer and probably saves material the mitre box.

dowel ¼ inch in from each end. It is here e edge of the bit should fall. You may, if you he middle, at ¾ inch from the dowel ends, bits are sometimes easier to edge-guide er-guide. That's one reason they're used need to drill about ½ the dowel depth at oint, and a Forstner bit starts more readily er point. Mark a longitudinal centerline on o, to facilitate drilling.

ind every dowel so each end has an arc one-heck the fit of the first few dowels and of a each wall stack as you go along; placing the one dowel in the arc of another should ypical log cabin look (Illus. 7–20).

the gable ends at 45 degrees, set them t the bottom to size. Then cut the bottom

5. The completed log cabin looks great, Bobby Weaver's patience and talent.

Paintbrush

Log Cabin Birdhouse

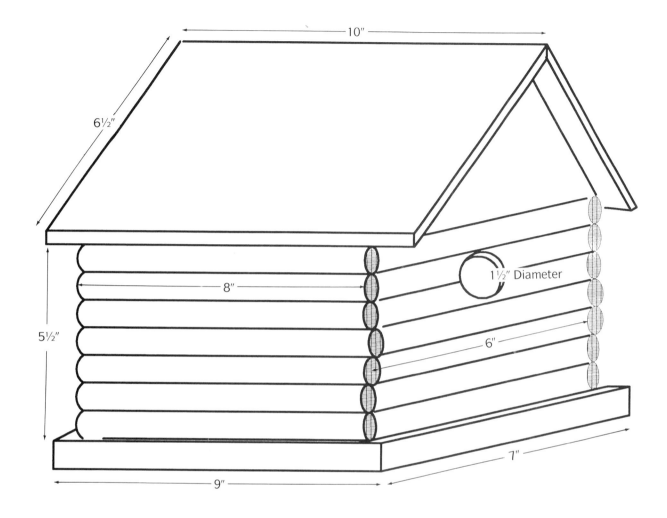

Illus. 7–16. Log cabin.

row of short dowels to half diameter. Split them right down the middle on a table saw or band saw; I greatly prefer a band saw for this kind of work. These half-round dowels do not have any arc cut. Set the first half-round dowel ½ inch in from the front of the floor and glue and nail it in place using 1-inch brads.

Use a pair of longer dowels to position the second half-round dowel, which should fall about ½ inch in from the other end of the floor. Glue and nail it in place, and then drive one nail down through the longer dowels into the dowel below, using finishing nails and the finish nailer.

While this project is possible using a hammer and finishing nails, it is much, much easier to use brad and finish air nailers. These nailers are expensive, but are great for fastening materials that otherwise require pilot holes; the dowels are standard birch, and nails do not drive well in such hard wood.

Use a standard square board end to maintain wall square as you nail the logs; you may also stand a square on its back and keep track that way. Do not try to eyeball the wall to determine if it is straight. The varying curves will fool you each and every time.

When you have reached the top, place the other half-round end pieces and finish nailing. Locate your entry hole in one end and place a piece of ¼-inch plywood over the spot. Tack-nailing such a support board in place makes it possible to drill a cleaner hole in the dowels in a situation where even a Forstner bit might "walk." Drill your 1⅛-, 1¼-, or 1½-inch hole.

Check the gable ends for fit, spread glue on the up-turned half-round dowels, and nail the gable ends in place. Then rip one piece of cedar clapboard to a 6½-inch width, and the other to 6¾ inches. Lay the narrower piece in place, after placing glue on the gable ends, and nail it in

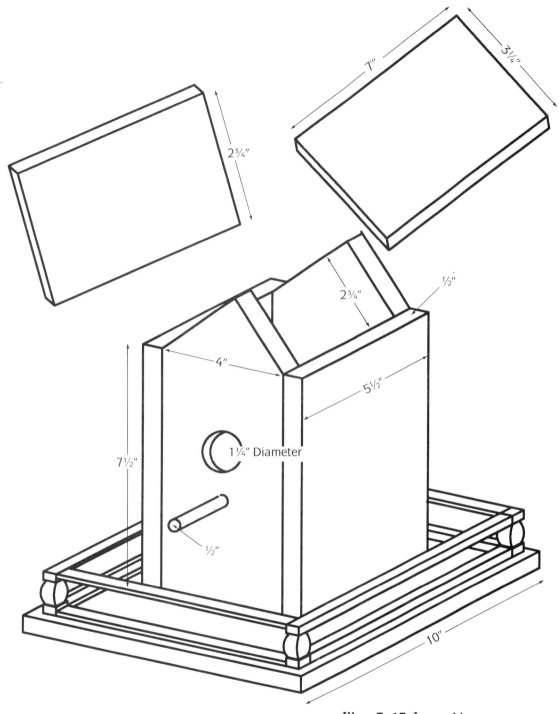

Illus. 7–17. Log cabin.

place. Overlap the top edge with the wider piece and finish glue nailing.

Sand the ends lightly, but don't do anything to the cedar roof. Coat the gable ends and the dowels, especially the dowel ends, with clear exterior polyurethane. Again, don't touch the roof. Bobby left the rough side of the cedar facing outwards on this cabin, and it is going to look fantastic as it ages.

This house installs easily; just drive a screw down through the floor into the top of a post, and reattach the roof to the house.

Illus. 7–18. A dowel jig for the cabin "logs."

Illus 7–19. A close-up of the jig shows a dowel not quite in position for drilling.

Illus. 7–20. Note the marks on the overall assembly in this close-up of the log cabin birdhouse. Bobby made sure that he didn't miss the needed spots.

STEEPLED BIRDHOUSE

Steeples usually denote public buildings or churches, and you may wish to add another symbol to this birdhouse to indicate which one your birdhouse is (Illus. 7–21 and 7–22). As built, it is a wren or chickadee house, depending on the size of the hole, but may also work as a birdhouse for a bluebird (1½-inch entry hole), tree swallow (1½-inch hole), titmouse (1¼-inch hole), and even a downy woodpecker (1¼-inch hole).

Materials

One piece of 2¾ × 3¼ × 7″ pine, for the *steeple*
Two pieces of 1 × 5½ × 10¼″ redwood, for the *front and back*
Two pieces of 1 × 4 × 8½″ redwood, for the *sides*. (For birds needing a larger floor space, make this 5½″ wide.)
One piece of 5½ × 7″ redwood for the *roof*
One piece of 4¾ × 7″ redwood for the *roof* (Both roof sizes will need changing if the floor space is expanded. If the floor space is being changed, make this roof 6¾ × 7″, and the roof listed above 7½ × 7″.)
One piece of 9 × 9″ pine or *redwood*, for the *floor*
⅜″ × 3″ diameter long dowel
Two 8 × 1¼″ square-drive screws with super-round washer heads, to make floor removable
¼ lb. 6d finishing nails or pneumatic brad nailer
Weatherproof wood glue
White enamel for steeple
Grey paint for floor

Tools

Circular, table, or other saw
Mitre box
Band saw, to cut steeple. (The steeple may be cut by hand, but the angles are too steep for a table saw or most mitre saws.)
Claw hammer (10 or 13 ounces)
Pneumatic nailer
Square
Measuring tape
2″-wide masking tape
Drill
1- or 1⅛″-Forstner drill bit
⅜″ drill bit
⅛″ drill bit (for pilot holes for screws)

Awl
Finish sander
Sandpaper (100 and 120 grit)

Instructions

Begin the work by cutting all pieces to their basic sizes as listed above. Next, cut the 45-degree angles at the 7½″ height on the front and back of the steeple. Such cuts are more accurate when you tape the two pieces together and cut both at the same time. Drill the entry hole—6½ inches up the front piece—and the dowel hole—3½ inches up the front piece—and get ready to assemble the birdhouse.

Bevel the sides so that the low side of the bevel is 7½ inches up the sides.

Next, place one side in a vise, and then dry-fit the front to the side. Apply glue to both pieces. Place three nails or brads to hold the pieces while the glue dries, and remove

Illus. 7–21. The completed steepled birdhouse.

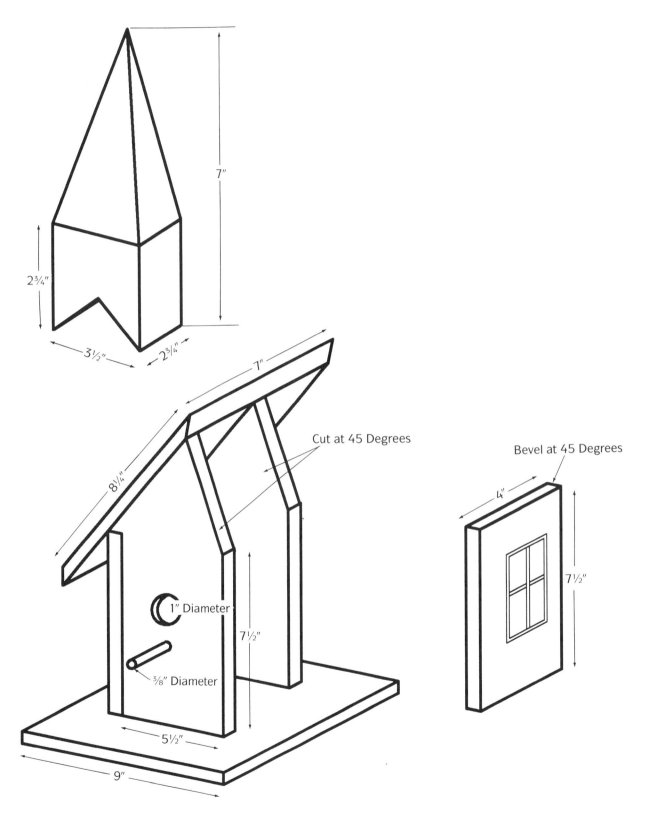

Illus. 7–22. The steepled birdhouse.

7"

2¾"

3½"   2¾"

7"

8¼"

Cut at 45 Degrees

Bevel at 45 Degrees

4"

7½"

1" Diameter

7½"

⅜" Diameter

5½"

9"

Birdhouse Plans

the assembly from the vise. Check the fit of the second side, and coat the side edge and the back of the front edge with glue. Use three more brads to hold the pieces while the glue dries. Set the assembly on its face and nail the back in place.

Mark an equal overhang for the front and rear of the roof section, and assemble the smaller roof section so that its top edge is even with the roof support edges of the front and back of the birdhouse; that is, the pieces should form a level surface for the next piece of roof, which should now be dry and should be installed. Install each piece with two brads or nails and glue.

Make the marks on the steeple for all cuts; mark only one side for each set of cuts. Set the band saw to cut to the proper depth. Make the first cuts on the shallower sides, and retain the scrap. Tape the scrap in place, and remark, if needed, the cuts on the deeper side over the tape. Reset the band saw depth of cut. Make those two cuts (Illus. 7–23).

Illus. 7–24. Test the fit of the roof-line cut.

Illus. 7–23. Tape the cut-off parts back in place and make the next cuts to finish up the steeple.

Hold the peaked steeple level against the roofline and mark the angle needed to fit the pieces. Check the marks, and then cut the pieces on the band saw (Illus. 7–24).

Next, sand and paint the floor and the steeple. Then sand the overall assembled unit, and finally install the perch dowel.

You have two options for the floor. The first is to cut a

Illus. 7–25. The steeple is installed with two brads (and glue) on each side of the base, so it is removable. If the roof side is to be removable, use two nails and glue on the removable roof side only. That way, the roof side and steeple will lift off as a unit.

second piece to fit inside the birdhouse, and mount the second piece to the original floor with brads and glue. Then attach the pieces to the sides with the square-drive screws; this makes a removable base that allows the birdhouse to sit level on any surface. Since I made mine for use on a fence or other post, I choose the second option. I just centered the birdhouse on the floor and ran in the two square-drive screws directly from underneath.

Once the floor is ready, you can make your choice. After that, install the steeple; I set mine back 1½ inches from the front roof edge for no reason other than that seemed like a good measurement—and so it proved. It looks fine (Illus. 7–25). You can increase the entry hole on this wren birdhouse to 1⅛ inches, so it will suit chickadees.

This house installs easily. Just drive a screw down through the floor into the top of a post, and then reattach the rest of the birdhouse to the floor.

FLAT-LOG CABIN

I decided this flat-log cabin (Illus. 7-26–7-28) would look great if made of walnut and lighter-colored woods in alternating strips. I was right, but had only short lengths of maple and ash. While cutting the maple on a table saw without the guards in place, I managed to twist the heel of the push stick so it caught a cut-off outside the blade, propelling the cut-off at me. It took a nice chunk out of my left hand and left a horseshoe-sized bruise on my right belly. Heed this warning from me: Woodworking is a great deal of fun, but it always has been, and will remain, potentially dangerous, even when you use common sense and all the guards correctly. Always remain alert and follow all safety procedures. I'll probably have to wait a month before resuming any truly active woodworking routine, but am otherwise unhurt, although angry at myself.

When you set up to cut the strips, make sure all guards are in place, and quit for a bit when you start to turn into an automaton. I discovered that I had enough strips to build two of these birdhouses, although I meant to build only one.

Materials

Eight pieces of ¾ × ¾ × 7½" walnut (or bubinga, purpleheart, or any other dark wood)
Eight pieces of ¾ × ¾ × 7½" oak (or maple, ash, or any other light wood)
Eight pieces of ¾ × ¾ × 4¾" walnut (or bubinga,

purpleheart, or any other dark wood)
Eight pieces of ¾ × ¾ × 4¾" oak (or maple, ash, or any other light wood)
Two pieces of 3½ × 7" scrap plywood, for the *eave ends*
Two pieces of 8 × 10" cedar clapboard, for the *roof*
One piece of 6¾ × 4" redwood or cedar, for the *floor*
One ⅜" diameter × 3" long walnut dowel
Two #8 × 1¼" square-drive screws with super-round washer heads
Weatherproof wood glue
Exterior satin polyurethane

Tools

Table saw
Mitre box
Claw hammer(10 or 13 ounces)
1¼ or 1½" Forstner bit
⅜" drill bit
⅛" drill bit for pilot holes for screws
Pneumatic nailer
Awl
Finish sander
Sandpaper (100 and 120 grit)
Paintbrush

Illus. 7–26. Alternating strips of walnut and lighter woods (ash, oak, and maple) make a good-looking cabin. There are all types of finish and wood combination possibilities for making this birdhouse.

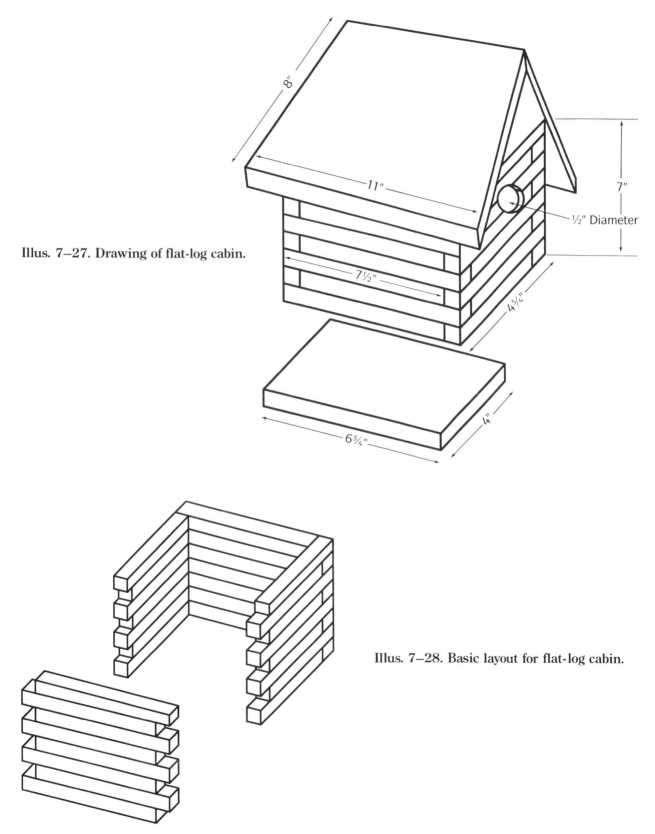

Illus. 7–27. Drawing of flat-log cabin.

8″

11″

7″

½″ Diameter

7½″

4¾″

6¾″

4″

Illus. 7–28. Basic layout for flat-log cabin.

Instructions

The first job is cutting the parts. This is easy enough, but first read my note on safety on page 62. As laid out, this birdhouse works well for titmice, but hole-size and height changes can make it suitable for chickadees or bluebirds, among others.

The assembly is easy, but time-consuming because of the number of parts and the need for care in laying them out. Anyone who decides to build more than two or three of these birdhouses definitely needs to assemble some sort of dual-corner jig to square the birdhouse as it is being assembled. I'd use opposing (diagonal) corners and set the jig to the final height of the birdhouse walls (6⅜ inches here), so that the entire unit could be assembled in the jig, and then lifted out. Make sure the jig walls are of a material that tends to reject wood glue, such as plastic (Illus. 7–29).

I started with a row of maple, changed to walnut, then to ash, then back to walnut, etc. That was simply more a matter of chance than design, and you may wish to use different arrangements of wood. Glue and nail layers until the walls are eight layers high; then take the eave parts and test-fit them. If they fit, place glue along the top edge of the end rows and use brads to nail the eaves in place.

Drill the entry hole. The plan shows a 1¼-inch entry hole for titmice. Drill the perch hole with the ⅜-inch bit, a couple of inches down from the entry hole.

Rip one piece of clapboard to a width of about 6 inches, and the other to 5¾ inches; lay the short one down first, gluing and nailing it in place, so that it is even with the top of the eaves. Lay the second piece down so that it overlaps the first one, and glue and nail it in place.

Drill the pilot holes for the screws that go into the bottom, and test-fit the bottom. Cut ⅜ inch off at least two of the corners of the bottom, for drainage. Remove the screws and bottom and finish the birdhouse after sanding the whole project lightly with 100- and 120-grit sandpaper.

I brushed on two coats of exterior satin polyurethane, with good results. Once that was dry, I replaced the bottom.

This house installs easily. Just drive a screw down through the floor into the top of a post, and reattach the birdhouse to the floor.

Illus. 7–29. Glue and nail the walls accurately, to ensure that they are straight. Use a Forstner bit to drill holes.

SMALL SALTBOX WITH OR WITHOUT A PORCH

I decided to make a saltbox birdhouse without a porch (Illus. 7–30 and 7–31). The primary difference between a saltbox with a porch and one without a porch is in the length of the front roof as it extends down over the front, the secondary base (there is no secondary base on the model I made), and the porch posts. If you like New England architecture, this birdhouse should pique your interest. The fact that it is made of white and red oak scraps and has a painted pine roof and bright-red chimney should also be of interest. The door and windows come from Meisel Hardware Specialty Store, and received a fast spray coating of green paint before being mounted.

Materials

Two pieces of 1 × 5½ × 9½″ red oak, for the *sides*
One piece of 1 × 2⁷⁄₁₆ × 9″ white oak, for the *back*
One piece of 1 × 7 × 9″ quartersawn white oak, for the *front*
One piece of 1 × 5⅜ × 7⅜″ quartersawn white oak, for the *bottom*

One piece of 1 × 10 × 6¾″ pine, for the *roof front*
(For the porch version add 2″, so you have a
1 × 10 × 8¾″ piece.) (Bevel the top 10″ edge at
45 degrees.)

One piece of 1 × 9 × 10″ pine, for the *roof rear*
(Bevel the bottom 10″ edge at 45 degrees.)

One 3¼ × 3½ × 1½″ chimney

Four dollhouse windows

One dollhouse door

Two #8 × 1¼″ square-drive screws with super-round
washer heads

#4 nails

⅝″ nails for doors and windows

Weatherproof glue

Red enamel

Grey flat paint

Green spray paint

Exterior satin polyurethane

1 × 11½ × 11″ base, to glue and nail to the bottom for
porch model, and two ½″ dowels, for *porch columns*

Tools

Table saw

Band saw or sliding compound mitre machine

Mitre box

Drill

1½″ Forstner drill bit

⅛″ drill bit for screw pilot holes

½″ drill bit if porch is added

Claw hammer (10 or 13 ounces)

Measuring tape

Square

Awl

Finish sander

Sandpaper (100 and 120 grit)

Instructions

Start by laying out the pieces to reduce waste, if you're
using anything other than scraps. Cut the sides and then
the front and back to full length. The bottom on my model
is made of red oak, but will serve better if made of cedar
or redwood. The roof is of rough-cut pine, and the chimney is a chunk off a 2 × 4, lightly planed to square up the
corners.

Cut the front angle on the sides to 45 degrees and
bevel the top of the front wall to match. Mark the back at
3 inches from its top and draw a line. I cut this angle on
the band saw. However, a sliding compound mitre machine will make the cut, *if* you place the already cut 45-
degree side against the mitre saw backboard. This is a
potentially dangerous process, though, because your fin-
gers are much too close to the blade. I seriously recommend the band saw or a handsaw.

Illus. 7–30. The front of this saltbox birdhouse is made of quartersawn white oak. This is true overkill for a birdhouse, but the piece was too small for anything else on hand. The roof is made of pine scraps, the sides and back of red oak, and the bottom (not visible) is hickory.

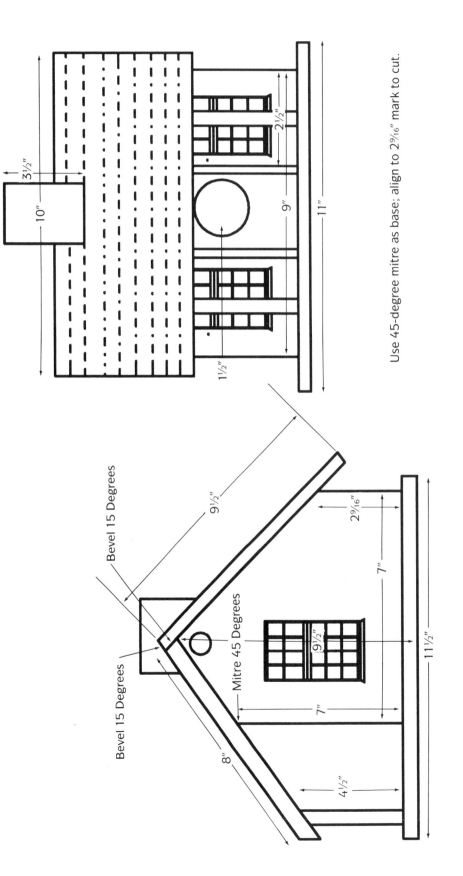

Use 45-degree mitre as base; align to 2⁹/₁₆" mark to cut.

Bevel 15 Degrees

Bevel 15 Degrees

Mitre 45 Degrees

Illus. 7–31. Saltbox birdhouse.

Set one side in the vise and check the fit of the 45-degree angles on its front and side. Remove the side and apply glue and nail it in place. Follow the same procedure for the next side. Place the back on the assembly and glue and nail it securely. Check the roof pieces for fit, and then glue and nail the front roof section so that its upper edges are even with the ridge.

Repeat the process with the rear section; then hold the chimney section level against the roof and draw your cutting lines. Make the cuts on the band saw.

Paint the roof and the chimney, making sure *not* to paint the underside of the chimney where it will be glued to the roof, and the part of the roof where the chimney will rest. When the paint is dry, glue and nail the chimney in place.

Drill for the entry hole. Then sand the whole project lightly with 100- and 120-grit sandpaper, coat it with exterior polyurethane, and place the doors and windows as you like. I centered the door so that the entry hole fit in the upper panel, and simply popped the windows in where I felt they looked best. I suggest you do the same.

The floor is attached with two of the #8 × 1¼-inch screws with super-round washer heads. This birdhouse installs easily. Just drive a screw down through the floor into the top of a post, and then reattach the birdhouse to the floor.

BASIC ADAPTABLE BIRDHOUSE

This medium-sized birdhouse (Illus. 7–32 and 7–33) can be readily adapted to fit most species that require more than a 4 × 4″ and less than a 8 × 8″ floor space. If you make it taller, it will fit most of the moderate-sized woodpeckers, as well as song sparrows, flycatchers, house finches, bluebirds, warblers, and a number of other birds. To adapt this birdhouse to accommodate a specific type of bird, check the entry-hole size required in the chart on pages 124 and 125, and drill a hole of that size. I built my birdhouse from cedar, using a couple of pieces of cedar clapboard for the roof; but you can use any wood you want.

Materials

Two pieces of 1 × 7½ × 9½″ cedar, for the *front and back*

Two pieces of 1 × 5½ × 6″ cedar, for the *sides*

One piece of 5½ × 6″ cedar, for the *floor*

Two pieces of 8 × 9½″ cedar clapboard. (Rip one to be ¼″ narrower than the other.)

One ⅜″ diameter × 3″ long birch dowel

Two #8 × 1¼″ square-drive screws with super-round washer heads

Illus. 7–32. This basic birdhouse is extremely quick and easy to make.

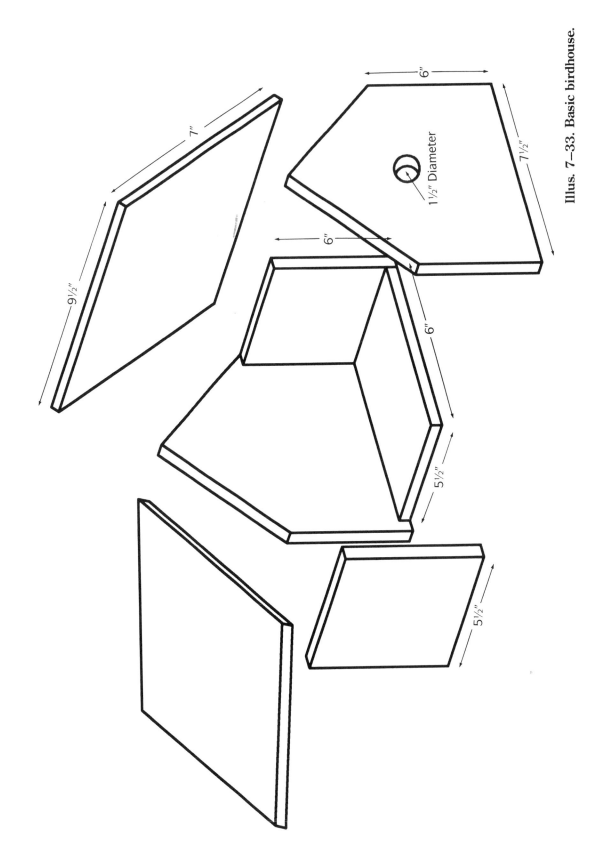

6"

7"

9½"

1½" Diameter

6"

7½"

6"

5½"

5½"

Illus. 7–33. Basic birdhouse.

Weatherproof wood glue
#4 galvanized finishing nails

Tools

Table saw
Mitre saw
Drill
1½″ Forstner bit
⅜″ drill bit
⅛″ drill bit for pilot holes
Claw hammer (10 or 13 ounces)
Pneumatic nailer (optional)
Awl
Finish sander
Sandpaper (100 and 120 grit)

Instructions

As always, cut the pieces to size. Rip the one piece of clapboard so it is ¼ inch narrower than the full-sized piece, and cut the 45-degree mitres on the front and back pieces.

Next, clamp and drill the front for both the entry hole and the perch dowel. Then begin assembly by checking the fit of one side against either the front or back. (Place the sides inside the front and back.) If both sides fit okay, glue the first side and nail it securely. Remove the assembly from the vise, add glue to the second side, and nail that side in place. With the project lying on its back, glue and nail the remaining front piece onto the sides.

Check the fit of the floor, and drill holes to accept the square-drive screws that hold it in place. Next, check the fit of the clapboard roofs. First, glue and nail the narrower piece in place, with its top edges aligning with the ridge. Then, glue and nail the last piece to the assembly. Finally, sand the whole project lightly with 100- and 120-grit sandpaper.

This is an all-cedar birdhouse, except for the dowel, and I didn't bother to add any kind of finish, because I'm curious as to how it will weather alongside all those I've already built that have different-type finishes.

This birdhouse installs easily. Just drive a screw down through the floor into the top of a post, and then reattach the birdhouse to the floor.

EASY-CLEANING WREN HOUSE

This house was easy to make in a small size, and my wife wanted some wren houses, so here it is (Illus. 7–34 and 7–35). It is one of the birdhouses I've made with exotic wood; it has a zebrawood roof, a Honduras mahogany front and back, and chestnut sides. The slide-out floor is made of cedar, and the handle of mahogany.

Materials

Two pieces of 1 × 5½ × 6″ Honduras mahogany, for the *front and back*
One piece of 1 × 5¼ × 7″ zebrawood, for the *roof side*
One piece of 1 × 4½ × 7″ zebrawood for the *roof side*
Two pieces of 1 × 4 × 4″ chestnut, for the *sides*
One piece of 1 × 1 × 5¼″ Honduras mahogany, for the pullout *floor handle*
One piece of ¼ × 4¼ × 5¼″ cedar, for the *floor*
Weatherproof wood glue
#4 galvanized finishing nails
Exterior polyurethane

Illus. 7–34. The completed easy-to-clean wren house looks good.

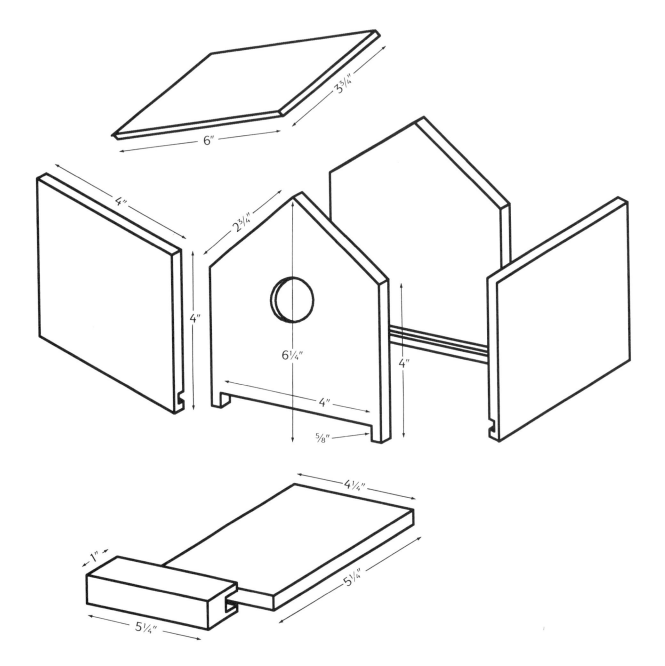

Illus. 7–35. Wren birdhouse.

Tools

Table saw
Dado set for the table saw (or ¼″ chisel)
Mitre saw
Band saw or scroll saw
Drill
1⅛″ Forstner bit
Claw hammer
Nail set
Square
Tape measure
Paintbrush
Finish sander
Sandpaper (100 and 150 grit)

Instructions

Begin by cutting pieces to their size. The front and back get 45-degree mitre cuts, starting 3⅜ inches up the side of each piece. Next, bevel the sides at 45 degrees, so that they fit inside the front and back. The front has to have a cutout 4⅜ inches wide by ⅝ inch high, to accept the dadoes and the slide-in floor.

Dado the bottom inside edges of the back and both sides, making a groove ¼ × ¼ inch and placing it ¼ inch up from the bottom of each piece. Also dado the front side of the handle. I suggest you dado this piece before you cut it from its main piece of stock, because it isn't large enough to hold on to. If you dado it *before* cutting it from the main piece of stock, use a very good push stick.

Glue the ¼″-thick floor and center it into the handle. Then drill the 1⅛″ entry hole (Illus. 7–36).

Start with one side in the vise, and assemble the front to the side, checking it first for fit, positioning of dadoes, etc. Make sure that the slot at the front of the birdhouse is going to be wide enough to accept the floor. It must slide freely.

Nail and glue the first side to the front; then remove the unit from the vise and nail and glue the second side. Turn the unit on its front and install the back with nails and glue. The roof goes on with the narrower piece just reaching the ridge, and the second piece overlapping the first piece. Both are nailed and glued in place. Sand the whole project lightly with 100- and 120-grit sandpaper (Illus. 7–37).

Check the fit of the slide-in floor and make any needed adjustments. Remove the floor and give the birdhouse two or three coats of exterior polyurethane—unless you've decided to use weather-resistant wood such as

Illus. 7–36. Clamp the front and use a Forstner bit to drill the entry hole.

Illus. 7–37. This is the finished assembly, seen from underneath. Note the dadoing.

cedar or redwood. I used polyurethane on this one simply to try to retain the look of the exotic woods longer. They're all pretty durable.

The result here is a truly unusual-looking wren house, but yours, too, may be unique because you'll possibly use different woods than I have.

Easy-Cleaning Wren House

CHICKADEE A FRAME

Chickadees are cheery little birds, and with patience can be enticed into feeding from one's hand. Those around where I live seem to spend most of their time chattering at me because I take too long to walk between our five feeders. In an effort to *increase* their waiting time, I'm putting out a number of chickadee nesting boxes this coming year, and this A frame is to be one (Illus. 7-38–7-40).

Materials

Two pieces of 1 × 8¼ × 6″ redwood, for the *roof*
Two pieces of 1 × 4¼ × 4¼″ redwood, for the *front and back*
One piece of 1 × 4½ × 4½″ cedar, for the *floor*
Two #8 × 1¼″ square-drive screws with super-round washer heads
#4 galvanized finishing nails
¼″ × 3″ diameter long cherry dowel

Tools

Table saw
Power mitre saw
Band saw
Claw hammer (10 or 13 ounces)
Pneumatic nailer
Drill
1⅛″ Forstner drill bit
¼″ drill bit
⅛″ drill bit for pilot holes
Finish sander
Sandpaper (100 and 120 grit)

Instructions

This little house has a couple of hard-to-cut oblique angles, which is why I include the band saw in the list of tools. It is much safer cutting angles on such small pieces on a band saw than on a table or power mitre saw.

Start by cutting the pieces to their final sizes, and then bevel the roof ridge at 45 degrees. Next, drill the 1⅛-inch entry hole in the front piece, and the ¼-inch perch dowel hole about an inch below the edge of the entry hole. That ¾-inch flat spot on the front and back pieces provides needed ventilation, so scribe lines from the lower corners to the ¾-inch mark; to do this, find the middle of the board and mark ⅜ inch to each side of the middle.

I found the easiest way to assemble this little birdhouse was to first put the roof together, cutting a single 30-degree bevel on one roof piece to fit onto the flat side of the other piece. Use glue and nails, but make sure you put the nails down an extra ¼ inch or so; if not, 1¼-inch brads will stick out the other side, and removing nails, even if you use an air nailer, is very difficult.

Next, mark the distance for the front and back pieces and glue and nail those pieces in place. Then test-fit the bottom, and drill the pilot holes for the screws. Place the bottom on the assembly, and attach the perch dowel with a dab of glue. Then sand the birdhouse lightly with 100- and 120-grit-sandpaper.

This house may be perched on top of a wood fence post (drive at least a 2-inch stainless steel screw down into the fence post) or mounted in other ways. I usually like to mount it into a 2 × 4 that is mounted on top of some plywood, which may then be screwed, nailed or otherwise fastened to almost anything. You might also hang the house using screw eyes and wire or chain; but I've got no idea whatever about whether or not chickadees will frequent a swinging birdhouse.

* * *

Illus. 7–38. Chickadee A frame birdhouse.

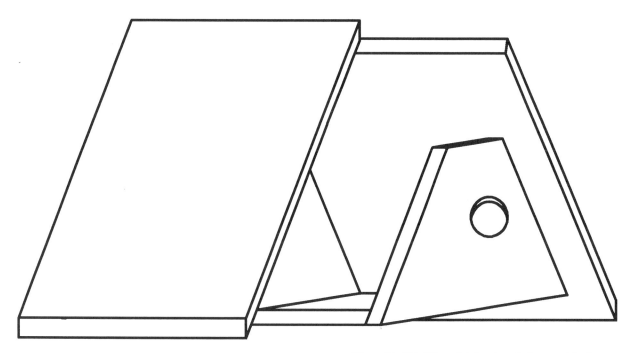

Illus. 7–39. The chickadee A frame birdhouse.

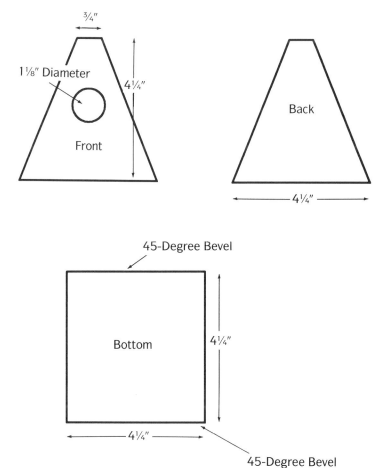

3/4"

1 1/8" Diameter

4 1/4"

Front

Back

4 1/4"

4 1/4"

Illus. 7–40. Bottom, back, and front parts for the chickadee A frame birdhouse.

45-Degree Bevel

Bottom

4 1/4"

4 1/4"

45-Degree Bevel

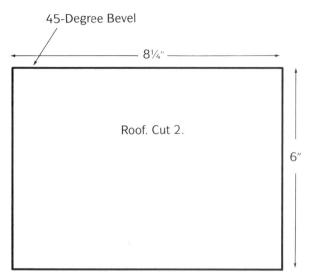

45-Degree Bevel

8¼"

Roof. Cut 2.

6"

Illus. 7–41. The roof for the chickadee A frame birdhouse.

ROBIN SHELVES

Robins like open-sided housing, where they can nest and retain interest in what the worms, and the rest of the world, are doing. This gang of three shelves does the job. The first two are super simple, while the last one needs a bevel cut (all of 10 degrees) and some band- or scroll-saw work.

The Simplest Nesting Shelf

This shelf (Illus. 7–42 and 7–43) can be set up just about anywhere. Keep in mind, however, that robins prefer to nest six to about 15 feet aboveground, so some house and barn eaves are ideal, while others are too high. I used pine for the shelf I built, but redwood may be more suitable.

Materials

One piece of $1 \times 9 \times 10''$ redwood, for the *roof*
One piece of $1 \times 8 \times 10''$ redwood, for the *back*
Two pieces of $1 \times 6½ \times 10''$ redwood, for the *sides*
One piece of $1 \times 7½ \times 9''$ redwood, for the *floor*
Two pieces of $1 \times 1 \times 6''$ redwood, for the *lower sides*
Weatherproof wood glue
#4 galvanized finishing nails
Wood filler
Enamel or clear finish

Tools

Table saw
Power mitre saw
Claw hammer (10 or 13 ounces)

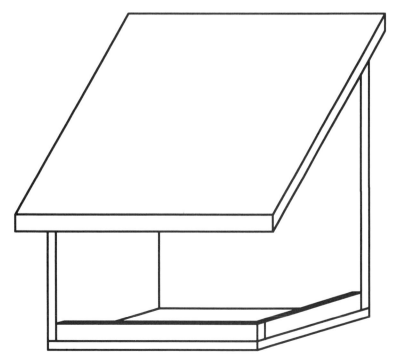

Illus. 7–42. The simplest robin nesting shelf.

Nail set
Measuring tape
Square
Pneumatic nailer
Finish sander
Sandpaper (100 grit)
Paintbrush

Instructions

Start by cutting all pieces to size. The back needs to have an angle matching that of the tall side cut (cut the tall side so that it angles from 10 inches long at its back to 8 inches at its front). Mark the bevel on the back and cut that next.

Begin assembly by attaching the back to the floor with glue and nails. Next, attach with glue and nails the single tall side, matching its bevels with the top of the back pieces. Now, nail on the lower sides, also using glue. Finally, position the roof in a manner that pleases you, and attach it using glue and nails. Mark carefully, to make sure you get the nails into the vertical pieces.

Finally, sand the robin shelf lightly with 100- and 120-grit sandpaper.

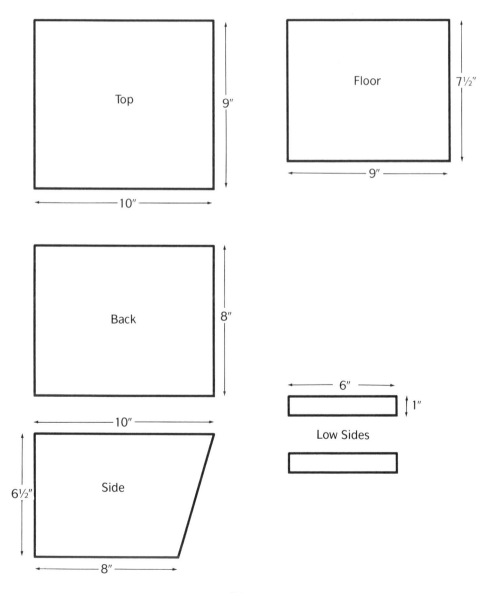

Illus. 7—43. Parts for the simplest nesting shelf.

Robin Nesting Shelve #2

This nesting shelf (Illus. 7–44 and 7–45) is actually a little simpler than the first, but it does require that you cut a curved line, although the single 10-degree bevel is very simple, and may even be eliminated.

Materials

One piece of 1 × 5 × 12½″ redwood, for the *roof*
Two 1 × 5½″ redwood squares, for the *sides*
One piece of 1 × 8¾ × 9¼″ redwood, for the *back*
One piece of 6½ × 7¾″ redwood, for the *floor*
Weatherproof wood glue
#4 galvanized finishing nails

Tools

Table saw or handsaw and plane
Mitre saw (optional)
Band or scroll saw
Claw hammer (10 or 13 ounces)
Nail set
Measuring tape
Square
Compass
1- or 2″-wide masking tape
Finish sander
Sandpaper (100 and 120 grit)

Instructions

Start by cutting all pieces to their finished sizes. Then use either the table saw, mitre saw, or a plane to bevel the top edge of the back (Illus. 7–46), tape the two sides together for pad-sawing, and cut it out with a scroll or band saw. Mark out the 2-inch radius curve on the front corner of the sides and cut it.

Begin assembly by placing the bottom in the vise and nailing one side to it. Do the same with the second side, out of the vise. Next, nail and glue the back to the bottom and sides.

Finally, center the top over the back and nail and glue it in place. Then clean it up with a finish sander and 100- or 120-grit sandpaper.

Illus. 7–44. Robin nesting shelf #2.

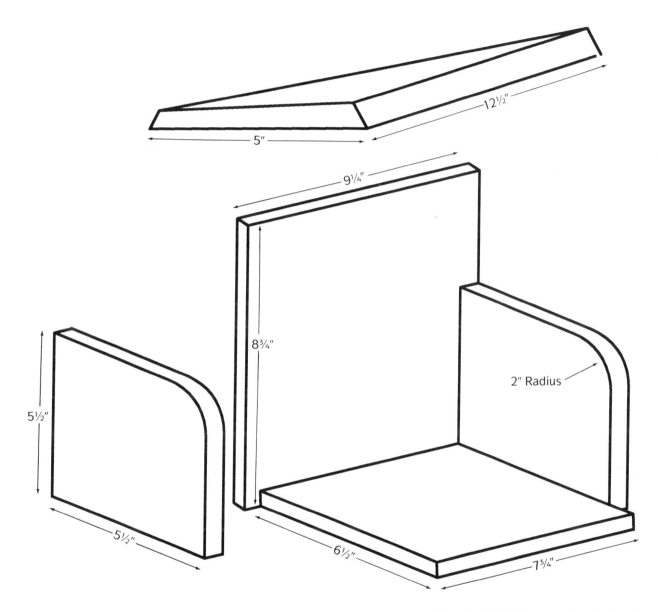

Illus. 7–45. Robin nesting shelf #2.

Illus. 7–46. The nesting shelf's back top bevel can be cut with a Jorgenson European pattern-cutting compound mitre machine.

Robin Shelf #3

Although it is more complicated than the other two, Robin Shelf #3 (Illus. 7-47–7-50) is not difficult. You do need to be careful gluing up the roof, because the way it is designed glue-nailing doesn't work, so you need clamps and a good glue line. Otherwise, it's all straightforward.

Materials

Two pieces of 5½ × 10″ redwood, one for the *roof*, one for the *floor*
One piece of 1 × 2 × 13″ redwood, for the *roof front*
Two pieces of 1 × 4¾ × 7″ redwood, for the *sides*
One piece of 1 × 7 × 10″ redwood, for the *back*
Weatherproof wood glue
#4 galvanized finishing nails

Tools

Table saw or handsaw and plane
Band or scroll saw
Oscillating spindle sander (optional, but helpful for this and other projects)
Two 10 or 18″ hand screws
Measuring tape
Square
2″-wide masking tape
Claw hammer (10 or 13 ounces)
Finish sander
Sandpaper (100 and 120 grit)

Instructions

This robin shelf is also a very easy project, requiring only careful layout and cutting for success. Begin by cutting the pieces to size and bevelling the front of the top.

Take the bevelled roof front and check its length against the other part of the roof. Open the hand screws to within a fraction of an inch of the size needed to grasp the two parts. Then spread glue carefully on both parts.

Illus. 7–47. Robin nesting shelf #3.

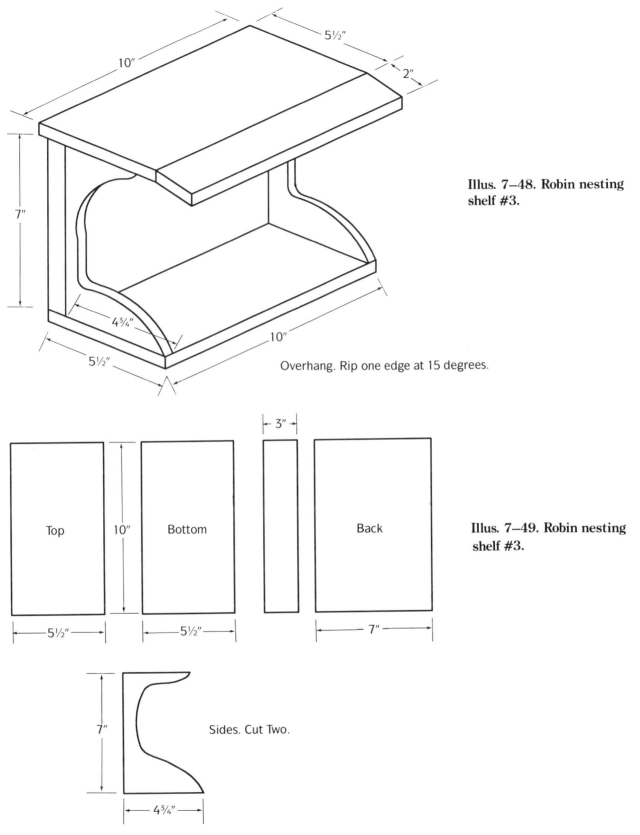

10"

5½"

2"

7"

4¾"

10"

5½"

Illus. 7–48. Robin nesting shelf #3.

Overhang. Rip one edge at 15 degrees.

3"

| Top | 10" | Bottom | Back |

5½"

5½"

7"

Illus. 7–49. Robin nesting shelf #3.

7"

Sides. Cut Two.

4¾"

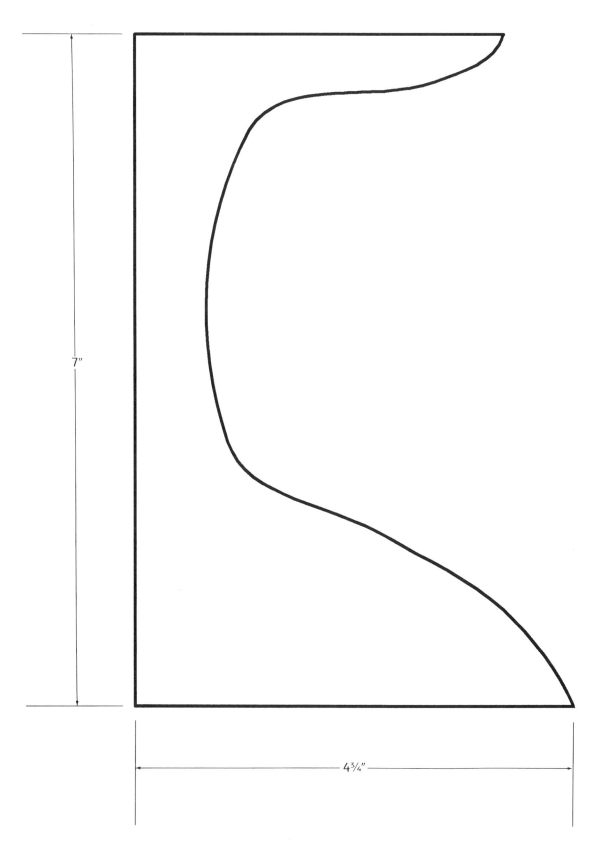

7"

4³/₄"

Illus. 7–50. Full-size pattern for shelf.

Birdhouse Plans

Wrap 2″ masking tape gently around the two mating pieces two or three times, to help prevent slippage. Then, with the roof on the bench, gently draw the tips of the hand screws around it, to provide light pressure. It is probably best to allow the clamped material to remain overnight, although I popped mine out of the clamps after about two hours and finished the project.

Using masking tape, tape the 4¾ × 7″ pieces together. Then make a copy of the pattern for the sides. Tape the pattern to the sides and pad-cut both sides on a band saw or a scroll saw (Illus. 7–51).

Begin assembly by nailing the back to the top of the bottom (place the back in the vise, spread glue, attach the two pieces and nail them). Next, sand the insides of the patterns and nail the side pieces. I love the little Ryobi oscillating sander for jobs like this. The work takes no time at all, and the sander does a truly good job of removing blade marks (Illus. 7–52).

Let the top dry before sanding it. Allow at least six hours of drying time, although it is preferable to let it dry overnight. Then apply glue to the tops of the back and sides and set the top in place. Align and nail the top.

Finally, sand the birdhouse lightly with 100- and 120-grit sandpaper.

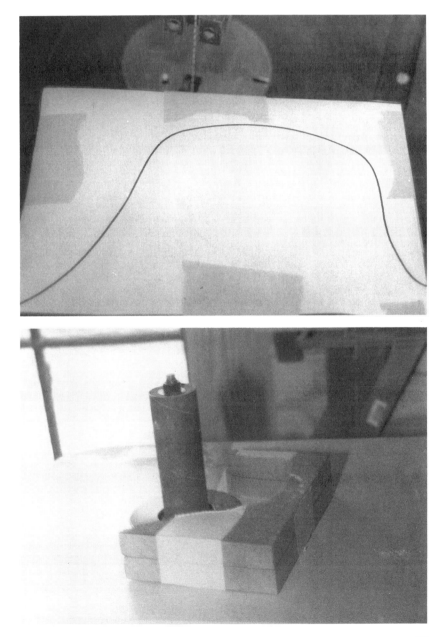

Illus. 7–51. Band-sawing the sides with the pattern taped to them, and the parts taped to each other, saves much time and trouble.

Illus. 7–52. Spindle-sanding the side parts is the easiest way to smooth their inside curves.

FLYCATCHER HOUSE

Flycatchers are small- and medium-sized birds found throughout the United States. In Virginia, where I live, the eastern kingbird seem to predominate, although the greater crested flycatcher is also known to live there. The smaller birds do well in houses suitable for bluebirds and nuthatches, with entry holes of 1¼ or 1½ inches, but the larger species need a specially sized flycatcher house (Illus. 7-53–7-55).

Materials

One piece of ¾ × 10 × 10″ plywood, for the *base*
One piece of 1 × 6 × 6″ pine, for the *floor*
Two pieces of ½ × 6 × 10″ pine, for the *sides*
Two pieces of 1 × 7 × 13″ pine, for the *front and back*
#4 galvanized finishing nails
Two #8 × 1¼″ screws with super-round washer heads
Weatherproof wood glue
Enamel finishes of choice. (I used red for the roof, white for the body, and blue for the base.)

Tools

Table saw
Power mitre saw
Drill
2″ Forstner drill bit
⅛″ drill bit for pilot holes
Claw hammer (10 or 13 ounces)
Nail set
Measuring tape
Square
Pneumatic nailer
Finish sander
Sandpaper (100 and 120 grit)
Paintbrush

Instructions

This is a simple project, although larger than most. The floor size is suitable for woodpeckers of several types, as well as the larger types of flycatcher. Change the entry-hole size to accommodate the woodpeckers: a 2½-inch entry hole for a flicker woodpecker; a 1½-inch hole for the hairy woodpecker; a 2-inch hole for the redheaded woodpecker; and a 2½-inch hole for the red-bellied woodpecker.

Begin by cutting the pieces to size, and then mitre the top of the front and back at 30 degrees. Also bevel the tops of the side and the long edge of both sides of the roof at 30 degrees.

Start the assembly by placing one side in a vise and gluing and nailing the front to that side. The sides fit inside the front and back. Remove from the vise to repeat the process with the next side; then glue and nail the back in place. With the box assembly complete, check the fit of the floor. If that fits, center it on the base, and glue and nail it in position.

Next, add the roof, with a 1″ overlap at the rear of the birdhouse (Illus. 7–56), using glue and nails.

If you wish to hang this birdhouse on a backboard, move the roof flush to the back wall and eliminate the base. Instead, cut a backer board 6 inches wide by 16 inches long from ¾-inch-thick stock, and use that as a fastening board.

Drill the 2-inch entry hole with its center about 6 inches up from the bottom of the house (Illus. 7–57). This height varies for different birds, including one or two woodpeckers, so you may want to raise the hole just about as far as it will go (in such cases, make the sides, front, and back at least 4 inches longer than specified in the plans, but retain all other measurements).

Illus. 7–53. This flycatcher house is red, white, and blue.

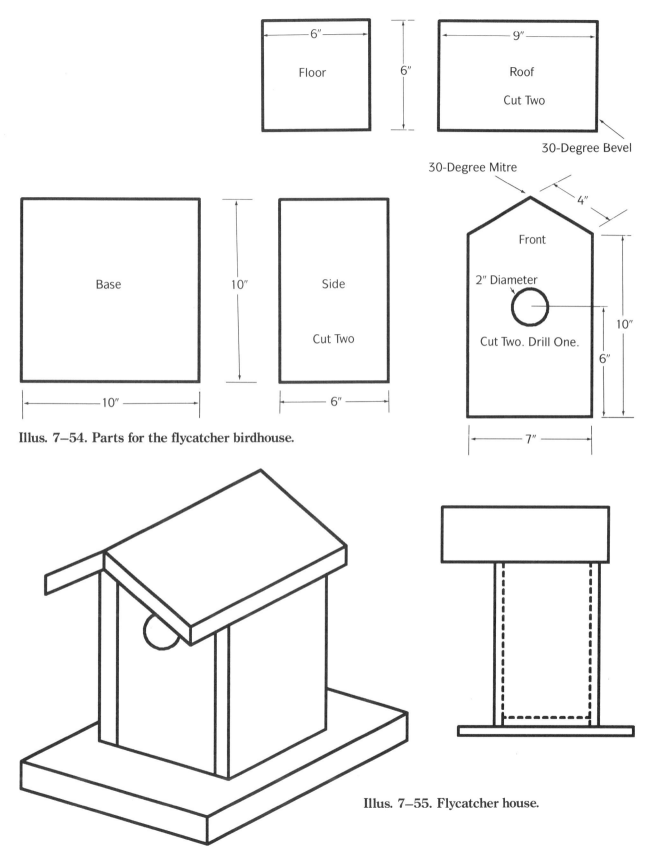

Illus. 7–54. Parts for the flycatcher birdhouse.

Illus. 7–55. Flycatcher house.

Illus. 7–56. Adding the roof to the house.

Illus. 7–57. Drilling the entry hole.

Install the floor and base and drill pilot holes for the two screws. Remove the floor and base and set the screws aside.

Sand the entire assembly with 100- and 120-grit sandpaper, and give it two coats of top-quality enamel finish in the color scheme of your choice.

CONCAVE ARCHED-ROOF WREN HOUSE

This little wren house (Illus. 7–58 and 7–59) can also be adapted for other birds. Chickadees also like birdhouses this size with the same 1⅛-inch entry hole. Changing the entry hole to 1¼ inches will entice nuthatches and titmice, among others. The arch and individual roofing strips give the house an unusual look, but don't add a lot of difficulty to the project.

Materials

Two pieces of 1 × 6 × 9½″ redwood, for the *front and back*

Two pieces of 1 × 4 × 4½″ redwood, for the *sides* (These sides need a top bevel of 30 degrees, or should be cut down to 3⅜ inches as shown in Illus. 2–63.)

One piece of 1 × 4⅜ × 4⅜″ redwood, for the *floor*

One ¼″ diameter × 3″ long dowel, for the *perch*

Fourteen 3⁄16 × 1¼ × 6½″ cedar strips, for the *roof*

Illus. 7–58. Concave, arched-roof wren house.

Two #8 × 1¼″ square-drive screws with super-round
    washer heads
#4 galvanized finishing nails
Staples for the roof
Weatherproof wood glue

Tools

Table saw
Band or scroll saw, to cut arch
Mitre saw
Drill

1⅛″ Forstner drill bit
⅛″ drill bit for pilot holes
Claw hammer (10 or 13 ounces)
Nail set
Measuring tape
Square
Vary Form tool, for marking arch
Pneumatic nailer
Pneumatic stapler
2-inch-wide masking tape
Finish sander
Sandpaper (100 and 120 grit)

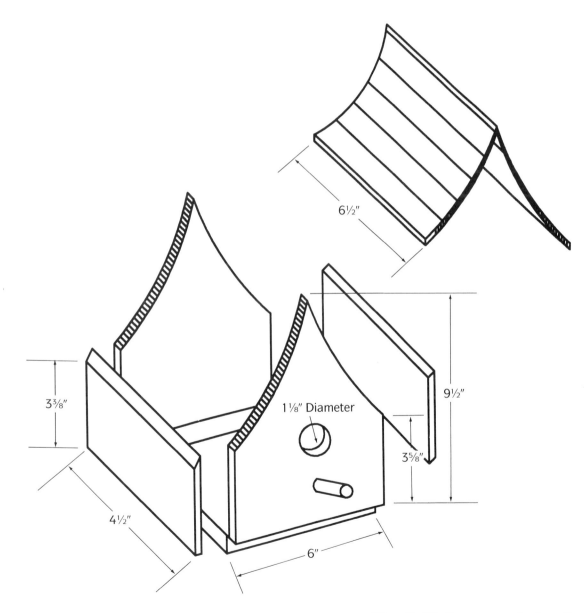

Illus. 7–59. Concave, arched-roof wren house.

Instructions

The roofing material on this birdhouse does require some extra work, although the rest of the birdhouse is simple to build. I ripped the needed material off some badly crushed cedar clapboard siding. You may wish to try getting some very thin cedar, redwood, cypress, or similar material and ripping pieces 1¼ inches wide (narrower pieces also work, but wider pieces don't because they break when forced into the curves) from available stock that you plane down to a thickness of ¼″ or less.

Start by cutting all the pieces to size, and then drilling the entry and the perch dowel holes in the front (Illus.

7–60). Use the Vary Form Curve Rule to mark a gentle concave curve from the middle of the front piece to the 3½-inch mark. I made the marks at the 5- and 11½-inch positions on the Vary Form Curve Rule, but you may prefer even less of a curve (Illus. 7–61). With much more of a curve, the roofing material tends to break as it is stapled in place. Tape the front and back together and cut the curves on the band saw or scroll saw (Illus. 7–62).

Assemble the front to one side, with the side held in a vise, using glue and nails. Remove the assembly from the vise and add the second side. Turn the project on its face and add the back. Check the fit of the bottom and cut each corner, ½ inch back from the edge, to 45 degrees, in

Illus. 7–60. As with all projects, carefully cut the parts of the arched-roof wren house to size before assembly.

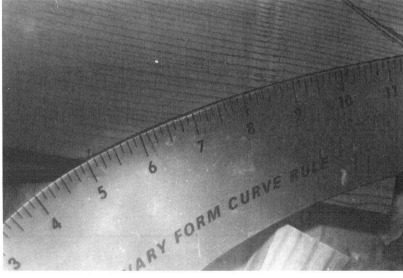

Illus. 7–61. Use a Vary Form Curve rule to mark the arch. Making marks at the 5- and 11½-inch positions on the rule gives the slight arch on the birdhouse.

Birdhouse Plans

Illus. 7–62. Cutting curves with the band saw.

order to promote drainage. Install the bottom using two #8 × 1¼-inch screws, set into pilot holes in the sides. This allows easy removal of the bottom, and the screws coming in from the side make it easy to put this birdhouse on a post without further modifications.

This birdhouse doesn't need any ventilation holes because the cedar-shingle overlaps provide plenty of gaps for air flow.

Check the fit of the cedar strips. If all is well, mark the curves at ¾-inch intervals, and staple the shingles in place. I didn't use glue here after the first shingles, until I got to the top, because the top seemed a bit loose. I applied three dabs of quick-setting epoxy to the top, and

then waited an hour before I sanded the house. After sanding, I glued in the perch dowel, and the house was ready for occupants.

Regardless of the more complex look, the hardest part of this project is stapling on the roof, and that takes only a few minutes once the roof is marked (Illus. 7–63). If you're going to work this kind of pattern for craft show sales, I'd suggest working out a jig to hold the shingles in place, reducing the need for marking each gable end individually.

This house installs easily. Just drive a screw down through the floor into the top of a post, and then reattach the birdhouse to the floor.

Illus. 7–63. The Campbell-Hausfeld lightweight stapler, for narrow staple heads, does a superb job of fastening the roof parts, if you remember to turn the air pressure all the way down to about 45 pounds.

NESTING HOUSE

This is an attractive, quickly built birdhouse (Illus. 7–64 and 7–65) that is suitable for any bird that requires a 4 × 4″ or slightly larger floor and a 1⅛, 1¼, or 1½-inch entry hole. This covers a range of birds from bluebirds to chickadees. The house is a little tall for wrens, but might prove acceptable in this case, too. The version you see here is built of red oak, with a paulownia top, mainly because I had a lot of red oak on hand and there was a small board of paulownia someone had sent me sitting around doing nothing useful. As indicated in the Materials list, however, you can use oak.

Materials

One piece of 1 × 7 × 7½″ oak, for the *roof*
One piece of 1 × 7 × 14″ oak, for the *back*
One piece of 1 × 4½ × 6¾″ oak, for the *front*
Two pieces of 1 × 5¾ × 8½″ oak, for the *sides*
One ⅜″ diameter × 3″ long dowel, for the *perch* (optional)
Five #8 × 1¼″ square-drive screws with super-round washer heads
Exterior polyurethane
#4 galvanized finishing nails
Weatherproof wood glue

Tools

Table saw
Mitre saw
Drill
1¼″ Forstner drill bit
⅜″ drill bit
⅛″ drill bit for pilot holes
Claw hammer (10 or 13 ounces)
Nail set
Measuring tape
Square
Pneumatic nailer
Finish sander
Sandpaper (100 and 120 grit)
Paintbrush

Instructions

Begin by cutting all pieces on the table and mitre saws. Then cut the mitre on the sides. This mitre is about 10 degrees, but you can merely align the 8½-inch lengths,

measure down 1½ inches on the front side, and make the cut that way. Bevel the back edge of the roof to 10 degrees for a tight fit at the back (Illus. 7–66).

Drill three or four ⅜-inch holes down the upper edge of each side, 1 inch in from that edge. Then begin assembly by glue-nailing one side to the back; set the side ½ inch in from the back's edge and 1½ inches up from its bottom, making sure its long side is against the back. Remove the unit from the vise, place the second side ½ inch in from the other edge, and glue-nail that in place. Place the roof in position on the sides and glue and nail it in place, with an equidistant overhang.

Drill the entry hole about 5 inches from the bottom of the front to the middle of the hole and drill, if desired, a ⅜-inch hole for the dowel perch about 2½ or 3 inches below that (Illus. 7–67). Place the front on the assembly and drill pilot holes for two screws about 1 inch down from the upper edge of the front. Screw them in and test the fit of the floor. Remove the floor and clip off its corners at 45-degree angles, cutting off about ½ inch of material (Illus. 7–68). You can attach the floor with removable

Illus. 7–64. Nesting birdhouse made of oak and paulownia.

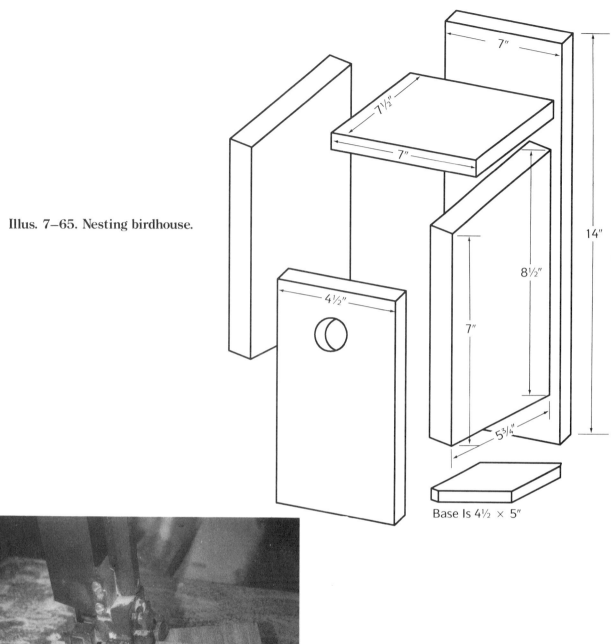

Illus. 7–65. Nesting birdhouse.

7"

7½"

7"

14"

8½"

7"

4½"

5¾"

Base Is 4½ × 5"

Illus. 7–66. Cutting the side-wall mitre on a band saw.

Illus. 7–67. The Forstner bits make an exceptionally clean-cut hole.

Illus. 7–68 (above left). Clip the floor corners, for drainage. Illus. 7–69 (above right). Coat the screws and other parts when adding a finish to the nesting box.

screws or use two or three brads in each side, plus glue. Do *not* drive brads through the front into the floor, and do not get glue on that edge. The front pivots, to allow the birdhouse to be cleaned out.

Sand the birdhouse carefully with 120-grit sandpaper, moving to 150 if you want a finer finish. Install the dowel perch, allow the glue on that to dry for at least a couple of hours, and then coat the birdhouse with exterior polyurethane (Illus. 7–69).

NUTHATCH CABOOSE

If you never got your fill of playing with trains as a kid, this birdhouse (Illus. 7–70 and 7–71) may be for you. It's the most complex one in this book, although it is not difficult to build. And I made it more interesting-looking by adding movable wheels and trucks, that is, the wheels spin on their axles and the trucks spin under the caboose, as they do on a real train. Otherwise, the details

Birdhouse Plans

are up to the builder. I added a roof cap for the cupola and the trucks to my birdhouse. This roof cap is not mentioned in the Materials list. You may use or delete the roof cap or trucks as you see fit. I used commercial wheels because I had some on hand. It is more economical, and maybe more realistic-looking, to use a hole saw to make 2½-inch-diameter wheels.

Materials

One piece of ¾ × 6½ × 12″ plywood, for the *roof*
One piece of ¾ × 6½ × 12½″ plywood, for the *floor*
Two pieces of ¾ × 6 × 10½″ plywood, for the *walls*
Four pieces of 1 × 4 × 6″ plywood, for the *sides and interior partitions* (partitions not shown in the drawing).
One piece of ¼ × 3 × 4½″ any wood, for the *door* (I used a scrap of walnut, and still feel guilty about painting it.)
One 1½ × 3 × 3″ block of pine, for the *cupola*
Two 1½ × 3½ × 4½″ blocks of pine, for the *trucks*
Eight 2½″-diameter wheels
Eight axles for the above wheels
Two 1½- or 2″-diameter wheels and axles
One ⅜″-diameter × 2½″-long dowel, for the *perch*
Three #8 × 1¼″ square-drive screws with super-round washer heads
#4 galvanized finishing nails

Wood filler
Red enamel finish
White enamel finish
Silver spray paint
Black spray paint

Tools

Table saw
Mitre saw
Drill
1¼″ Forstner drill bit
¼″ bit for small axle holes that hold truck to body
⅜″ bit for dowel and axle holes
⅛″ drill bit for pilot holes
Claw hammer (10 or 13 ounces)
Nail set
Measuring tape
Square
Pneumatic brad nailer
Laundry marker, to draw cupola windows
Finish sander
Sandpaper (100 and 200 grit)

Instructions

Cut all pieces to their listed sizes (Illus. 7–72) and then check them for square. Start the assembly by aligning

Illus. 7–70. The nuthatch caboose.

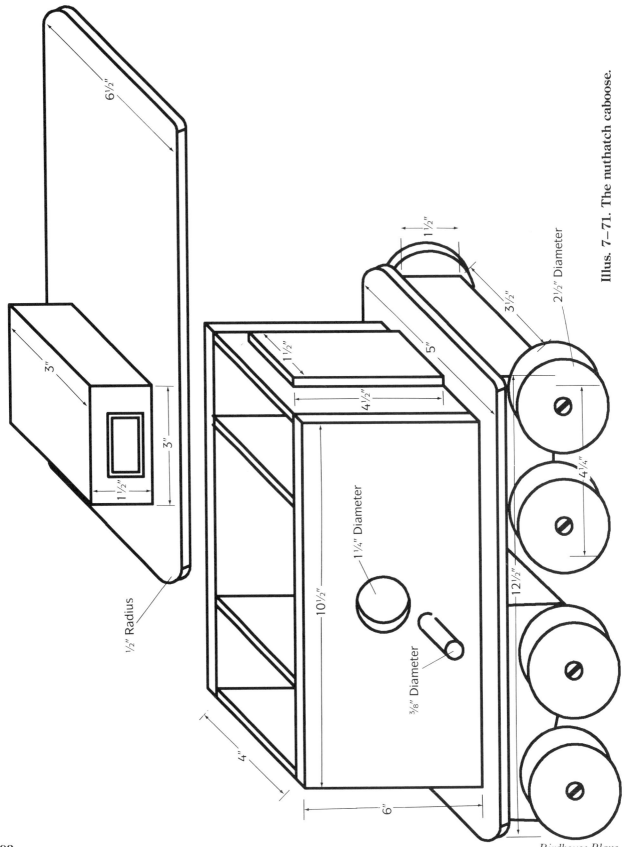

6½"

½" Radius

3"

3"

1½"

1½"

4½"

10½" Diameter

1¼" Diameter

3⁄8" Diameter

4"

6"

5"

3½"

1½"

2½" Diameter

4¼"

12½"

Illus. 7–71. The nuthatch caboose.

Illus. 7–72. Cut all pieces to size. For general use, this Stanley Short Cut finish saw is excellent.

the sides to the edges and front of the caboose (although the drawing shows the floor overlapping the assembly, check Illus. 7–70, for it does *not* overlap). Drill the entry hole and the hole for the dowel perch on the front piece, and then glue and nail the front to the assembly. Glue and nail the back in place after drilling three or four ⅜-inch ventilation holes 1 inch below the upper edge.

Place one partition so that it is 1½ inches in from the left end, and the other so that it is 2¾ inches in from the right end. These partitions reduce the oversized compartment, to make it more comfortable for small birds (Illus. 7–73). Then fill all nail holes, and sand the body.

Construct the cupola by positioning it about 1½ inches in from the front end, centering it, and gluing and nailing it (it is a piece of 2 × 4 that has been planed down). You'll need to drive the nails in from the underside of the top. Then sand it lightly (Illus. 7–74). It simplifies things if you paint the block sides red and draw the windows on before mounting this part. I added a 4 × 4-inch cap of scrap redwood, painted silver, to finish things off, painted both cupola sides and then the roof, and then drew the windows. Then I assembled it, making a messier job than I'd have liked.

Set the assembled roof aside or tape off the cupola and cap and spray the top silver at this point. You'll need at least two coats, maybe three, so starting early is a good

Illus. 7–73. Partitions are added to reduce the size of the inside.

Illus. 7–74. Finish the roof and cupola.

idea. While you're painting, paint the wheels, axles, and trucks flat back, making sure to keep the parts to be glued free of paint. I taped the most important parts (Illus. 7–75).

Locate the middle of the underside of the floor and position a hole, locating it about 3 inches in from the front (blank end) and 4 inches in from the rear. Then drill a ¼ × ½"-deep hole to accept the small axle. This is where the trucks go.

Build the trucks next by locating holes ½ inch in from each end of each truck on both sides of each truck, and ⅝ inch up from the bottom. Drill ½" deep × ⅜" diameter holes (Illus. 7–76). Next, take the small (1½ or 2") wheels and one axle for each wheel, center them on the tops of the trucks, with the normal outside edge down, and insert the axle (the axle is inserted so it will be trapped by the truck). Glue and nail, using 1-inch brad nails, each wheel into position. Once four wheels are added, the unit will pivot on these axles, which are eventually glued into the hole in the bottom of the caboose floor.

Insert the axles in the other wheels, dab glue on ½ inch of the axle ends, and drip a little glue into the holes. Insert the wheels and axles into holes in the trucks, and tape them tightly. Let them dry for at least one hour, preferably for several hours.

Paint the body of the caboose red, the back door white, the roof silver, and the step floor back. Then, invert the topless caboose and place the truck pins into the corresponding holes in the underside of the floor, after coating the pins' ends (about ⅜ inch) and the inside of the hole with glue.

Allow the assembly to stand until the glue has set and nearly cured—at least two hours. Then stand the caboose on the wheels, align the roof, and drill the pilot holes for the #8 × 1¼-inch screws that hold the roof in place. The three screws make the roof removable for cleaning.

Illus. 7–75. The partly assembled and sprayed trucks. Tape on the axle-peg ends to ensure that they'll adhere properly later. Smaller wheels are glue-nailed in an inverted position, with the axle-peg head trapped under the wheel. Do *not* glue the axle peg.

Birdhouse Plans

Illus. 7–76. The assembled truck shows the inserted clean axle end that goes up through the holes in the floor.

HEART-FRONT BIRDHOUSE

Hearts are an "in" decoration these days, so here's a simple birdhouse for titmice, white- and red-breasted nuthatches, and downy woodpeckers, with the hopes the heart beat will draw breeding families (Illus. 7–77 and 7–78). The pattern included is full-sized, to make things easier.

Materials

One piece of 1 × 7½ × 8″ pine, for the *heart*
Two pieces of 1 × 5½ × 5″ pine, for the *front and back*
Two pieces of 1 × 4 × 5″ pine, for the *sides*
One piece of 1 × 6 × 6½″ pine, for the *roof*
One piece of 1 × 4 × 4″ pine, for the *floor*
⅜″ diameter × 3″ long dowel, for the *perch* (optional)
#4 galvanized finishing nails
Two #8 × 1¼″ square-drive screws with super-round washer heads
Weatherproof wood glue
Red water-based enamel finish
White water-based enamel finish
Wood filler

Tools

Table saw
Band saw with scrolling blade or scroll saw
Handsaw
Mitre saw

Drill
1¼″ Forstner drill bit or hole saw
⅜″ drill bit, for *perch dowel hole* (optional)
⅛″ drill bit for pilot holes
Claw hammer (10 or 13 ounces)
Nail set
Measuring tape
Square
Pneumatic nailer
Finish sander
Sandpaper (100 grit)
Paintbrush

Instructions

Start by laying out and cutting all the square pieces; then check the cuts to make sure the parts are square. Find the location of the entry hole on the piece of wood that will have the heart pattern, and mark its middle (at least 3 inches from the bottom of the birdhouse to the lower lip of the hole is needed). Also locate the hole for the perch dowel, which you may drill now if you wish. Do *not* drill the entry hole yet, as that needs to be drilled through both layers. Lay out the heart pattern on its workpiece and tape it down. (When I'm building these types of project I print extra patterns on my laser printer, but a copier can also be used. This way, you've always got an original to work with later. Use the first cutout as a pattern for the rest, if you're making more than one). Then cut the heart, and sand the edges carefully. Next, paint the heart and allow it to dry.

Assemble the box by placing one side in the vise and

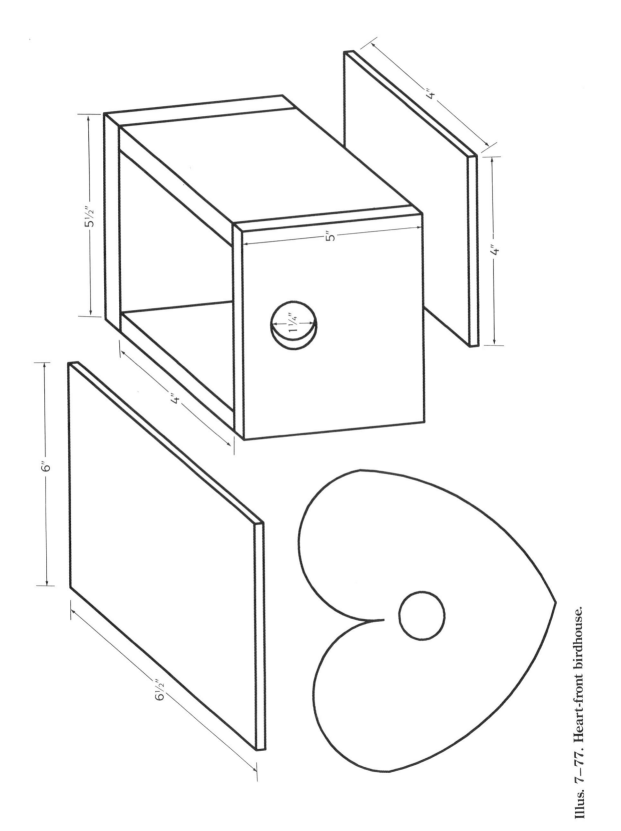

5½"

5"

1¼"

4"

4"

4"

6"

6½"

Illus. 7–77. Heart-front birdhouse.

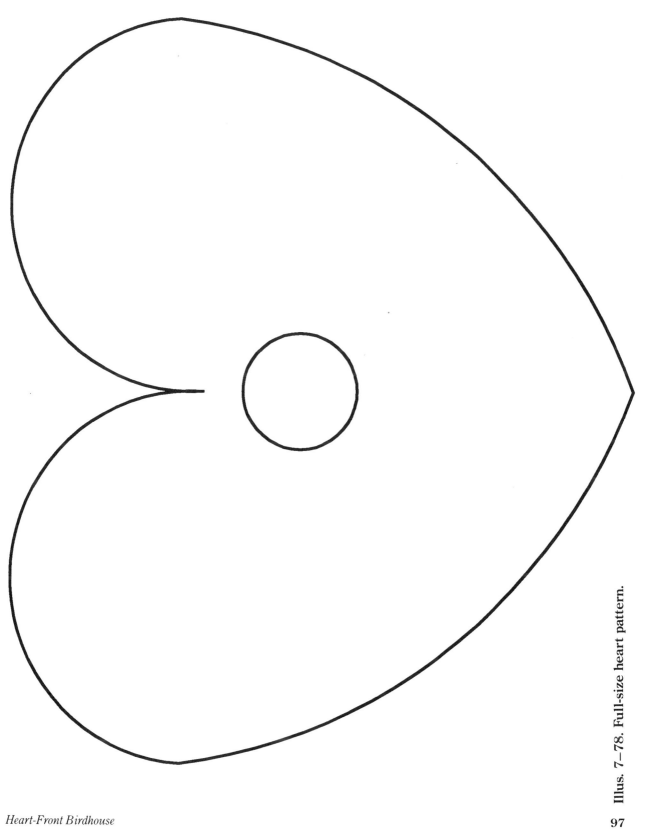

Illus. 7–78. Full-size heart pattern.

aligning the front with it, gluing and nailing the front in place. Remove the assembly from the vise and attach the other side with glue and nails. Flip the assembly onto its front and attach the back, keeping the box square. Insert the bottom to check its fit; it should fit fairly loosely. Drill pilot holes and temporarily assemble the bottom with square-drive screws, one in each side.

Now, sand and paint the box your choice of colors; I've listed white, but any color is fine. Make sure to remove the floor before painting the birdhouse, unless you want the screws the same color as the basic house.

Place the heart on the front of the birdhouse box. Glue and nail it there. Make sure you keep nails out of the area you'll be drilling for the entry hole.

Even with glue and nails, give the front a couple of hours to dry before drilling the entry hole. That's not because it needs the structural help of set glue, but to keep wet glue from getting on your Forstner bit, which is not good for the tool, even though the amount transferred is minimal. Drill the hole and paint the inside edges.

Next, glue and nail the roof in place. Then check for any touchups needed on the paint and place your new birdhouse in the correct location, to draw the species you want.

TITMOUSE HAVEN

This is the house that led me to search for different kinds of wood amidst the scrap pile. I had one piece of purpleheart, some oak, and some other woods, so seeing what it all looked like combined in a small project appeared to be a good idea. Certainly, it is different (Illus. 7-79–7-81).

Materials

Two pieces of 1 × 6 × 10½″ purpleheart, for the *front and back*
Two pieces of 1 × 4½ × 5½″ oak, for the *sides*
One piece of 1 × 4 × 4½″ oak, for the *floor*
One piece of 1 × 6¼ × 7″ redwood, for the *roof*
One piece of 1 × 7 × 7″ redwood, for the *roof*
One piece of ⅜″ diameter × 3″ long dowel, for the *perch*
#4 galvanized finishing nails
Two #8 × 1¼″ square-drive screws with super-round washer heads
Weatherproof wood glue

Tools

Table saw
Mitre saw
Drill
1¼″ Forstner drill bit
⅜″ drill bit, for dowel for the *perch*
⅛″ drill bit for the pilot holes
Claw hammer (10 or 13 ounces)
Nail set
Measuring tape
Square
Pneumatic nailer
Finish sander
Sandpaper (100 and 120 grit)
Paintbrush

Instructions

Make the 50-degree mitre cuts on the front and back immediately after cutting all pieces to size. Not all mitre

Illus. 7–79. Titmouse haven.

saws, power or hand, will open out this far, but my Ryobi 8½″ sliding compound mitring machine does, as does my Makita saw. In fact, the Makita will take the cut out to 55 degrees if needed. Bevel the roof halves about 20 degrees, and overlap them at the peak during assembly.

Cut the lower taper on the front and back simply by marking the ½-inch taper and using a handsaw or band saw to rip it off.

Drill the ⅜-inch perch dowel and 1¼-inch entry holes in the front, placing the larger hole's middle 6 inches up from the bottom of the front, and centering it. The dowel perch goes at about 2 to 3 inches from the bottom, and is, of course, centered.

Place one side in the vise and glue and nail the front to it, keeping the outsides flush and the bottoms of the side and the front even. Remove the assembly from the vise and repeat the process with the other side; then glue and nail the back in place.

Next, stand the unit upright and install the roof, letting it overhang the front ⅝ to ¾ inch; place the shorter roof piece first and then overlap it with the longer piece. Then check the fit of the floor—as with all birdhouse floors, too tight a fit isn't a good idea. I clipped the corners of my floor at 45 degrees, and made sure the floor still fit loosely. Drill pilot holes for the #8 × 1¼-inch screws and set the birdhouse aside.

Glue in the perch dowel. Now, sand the entire unit lightly. Then coat the birdhouse three times with exterior polyurethane, sanding it after each coat.

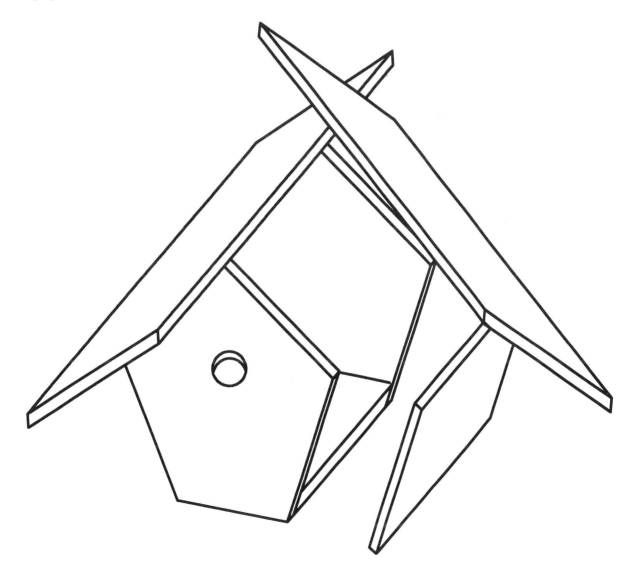

Illus. 7–80. Titmouse haven.

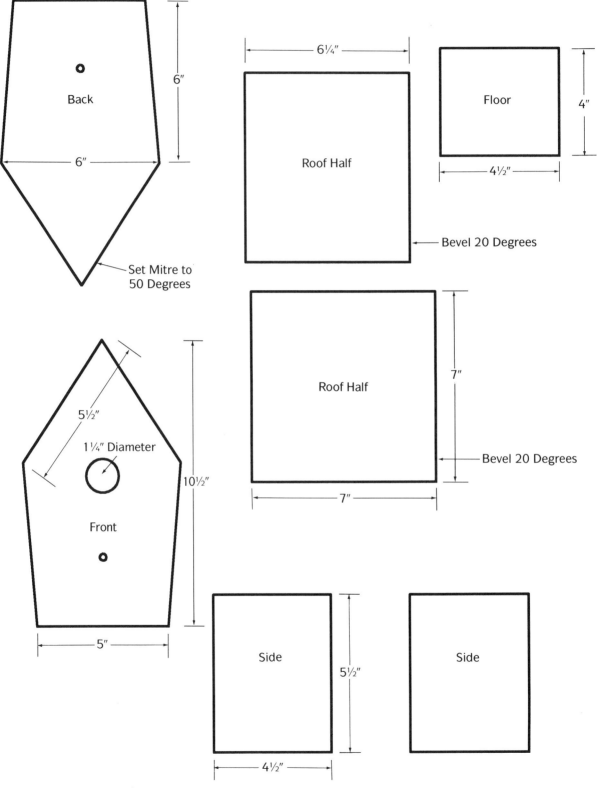

Illus. 7–81. Titmouse haven.

ADOBE MARTIN HOUSE

Of course, this house is no more made of adobe than I'm a teenager, but it *looks* like an adobe dwelling (Illus. 7–82 and 7–83). It is the largest project in this book, though not the most difficult. The construction is primarily straightforward, and the unit goes together quickly. Martins are useful birds, gobbling thousands of insects a day, so are considered a good omen in a neighborhood.

Materials

One piece of ¾ × 14½ × 24″ plywood, for the *front*
One piece of ¾ × 13¼ × 24″ plywood, for the *back*
One piece of ¾ × 12 × 24″ plywood, for the *base*
One piece of ¾ × 8⅜ × 8¾″ plywood, for the *middle-section tower*
One piece of ¾ × 6½ × 7″ plywood, for the *second floor in the middle-section tower*

Two pieces of ¾ × 8¾ × 8¼″ plywood, for the *side wing roofs*
Two pieces of ¾ × 14¼ × 7″ plywood, for the *middle-section side walls*
Twenty-two ⅜″ diameter × 1½″ long dowels, for *imitation joists*
#4 galvanized finishing nails
Weatherproof glue
Sand-colored flat paint
Gloss brown paint
Four #8 × 1¼″ square-drive screws with super-round washer heads

Tools

Table saw
Handsaw
Band saw
Mitre saw
Drill

Illus. 7–82. Adobe martin house.

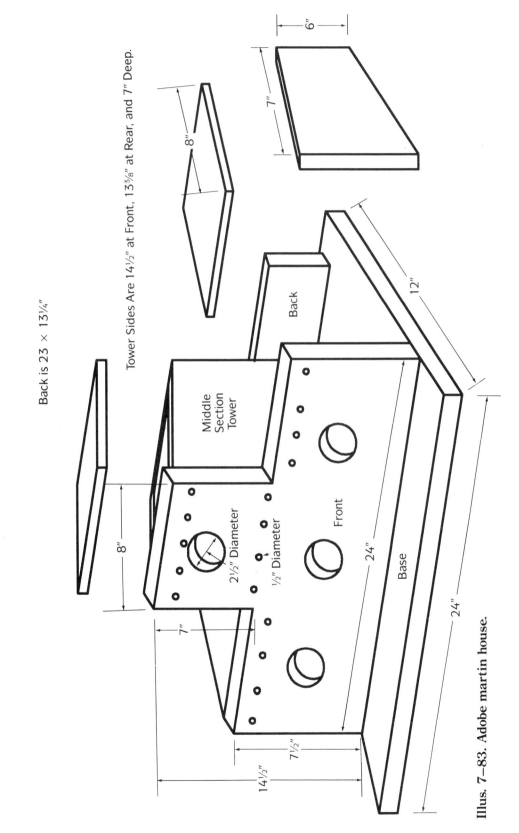

Back is 23 × 13¼"

Tower Sides Are 14½" at Front, 13⅜" at Rear, and 7" Deep.

6"

7"

8"

Back

Middle Section Tower

12"

8"

2½" Diameter

½" Diameter

Front

24"

Base

24"

7"

7½"

14½"

Illus. 7–83. Adobe martin house.

2½″ Forstner drill bit or hole saw
⅜″ drill bit, for dowels
⅛″ drill bit, for pilot holes
Claw hammer (10 or 13 ounces)
Nail set
Measuring tape
Combination square
Pneumatic nailer
Finish sander
Sandpaper (100 grit)
Paintbrush

Instructions

For this birdhouse, I made the back removable, because that was the simplest way to get to all four rooms to clean them. Start by cutting all pieces to rough size, including the front and back; then drill the entry and perch holes (Illus. 7–84).

The front and back of this martin house provide some challenge. Cut a 10-degree bevel on the front, back, and sides of the birdhouse. I found it far more sensible to use a band saw to make the cutouts that formed the tower. Tilt the table and make the bevels as you make the cutouts. I tried to make the cutouts on one side with the table saw and tore up some wood for my troubles. The table saw is terrible for this sort of interior work that has to be lifted off and lowered onto a moving blade. The band saw is much better. In fact, so is a handsaw.

Lay out the four rows of ⅜-inch holes with a combination square and a scriber or pencil as shown or as you

please. The drawing shows ½-inch-diameter dowels, but I had none, so worked with what I had.

With the rough sizes ready, cut the mitres on the ends of the front, running them from 7½ inches high down to 6 inches. Use a band saw, handsaw, or a mitre box for these cuts.

Cut the mitres on the back in the same manner as the front, but about ⅛ inch lower overall. The rest of the drop is taken care of when the back is set in place level with the *bottom* of the base.

Next, start the assembly with the two inner walls, gluing and nailing those to the front. Place the middle floor and glue and nail that in place, too.

Next, glue and nail the two ends in place, and check the roof to see if it fits. Glue and nail the roof in place. Next, upend the assembly and add the bottom, gluing and nailing it, too (Illus. 7–85).

For the back to remain removable, you need at least four screws, two going into each end wall and two or more into each middle tower wall. Drill pilot holes after checking the fit of the back. Install the back, and then remove it, to prepare it for painting. Then sand the entire unit lightly with 100-grit sandpaper.

Next, wrap ½ inch of masking tape on the ends of the dowels and spray-paint them with the brown paint. Use the sand-colored paint to coat the overall martin house, giving it an intense adobe look (Illus. 7–86).

Set the dowels in place after dipping the end of each in glue. Then reinstall the back after mounting the martin house on a pole. Martins like to nest at least 15 feet off the ground.

Illus. 7–84. The drilled holes in the front.

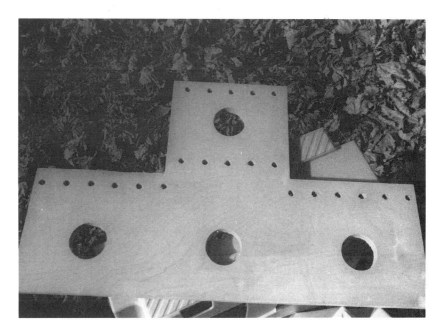

Illus. 7–85. The assembled front shows the walls and roofs.

Illus. 7–86. 3M's disposable NewStroke brushes are ideal for this kind of rough painting.

BIRDHOUSE WITH PORCH

Porches add to the character of any birdhouse, and this birdhouse looks good, with or without the porch. The 1¼-inch entry hole can be modified to suit other birds that prefer a small birdhouse, and construction is very simple (Illus. 7–87).

Materials

Two pieces of 1 × 5¾ × 8″ cedar or redwood, for the *front and back*

Two pieces of 1 × 4¼ × 5″ cedar or redwood, for the *sides*

One piece of 1 × 5¼ × 9″ cedar or redwood, for one section of the *roof*

One piece of 1 × 6 × 9″ cedar or redwood, for one section of the *roof*

One piece of 1 × 4¼ × 4¼″ cedar or redwood, for the *floor*

One piece of 1 × 9 × 9″ cedar or redwood, for the *base*

Two 1 × 1 × 7″ wood strips or ¾″ diameter × 7″ long dowels, for the *porch posts*

#4 galvanized finishing nails

Two #8 × 1¼″ square-drive screws with super-round washer heads

Wood glue

Tools

Table saw

Handsaw

Band saw

Mitre saw

Drill

1¼″ Forstner drill bit or hole saw

⅛″ drill bit for pilot holes

Claw hammer (10 or 13 ounces)

Nail set

Measuring tape

Square

Pneumatic nailer

Finish sander

Sandpaper (100 grit)

Instructions

First, cut all pieces to their sizes indicated in the Materials list, and then add either two strips of 1 × 1 × 7-inch wood strips or two ¾-inch-diameter, 7-inch-long dowels for the porch posts. Next, drill the 1¼-inch-

diameter entry hole about 4¼ inches up from the bottom of the front. Cut the mitres on the front and back, using a 45-degree angle in the mitre box.

Using glue and nails, attach one side to the front, with the side clamped in a vise. Remove the unit from the vise and repeat the process for the second side, with the front resting on the two sides. Glue and nail the back to the sides, with the assembly resting on the front.

Next, check the size of the opening for the floor, and make sure the floor fits easily. Center the floor on the base and glue and nail the two parts together. Then attach the shorter section of the roof, aligning it with the ridge line. Glue and nail it in place, making certain that there is at least 2½ inches of overhang in front. Do the same for the second piece of roofing, and then set the entire assembly down on the floor. Drill pilot holes for two square-drive screws so they go through the lower sides of the house and into the floor. Run in the screws.

Next, add the porch posts. There are different procedures for the posts, depending on whether you want to use wood strips or dowels. The strips use glue only, and are the simplest to install. Begin by holding the base of the post flush on the base, and mark the angle at the roof line. Cut the angle and test the post. If it fits, cut the second piece in the same manner.

Coat the ends of the posts with glue and slip them into place, forcing them very slightly so that there's enough pressure to hole them while the glue sets.

If you decide to use ¾-inch dowels, the procedure is similar, with one major difference: Hold the 7-inch-long dowel section against the porch to get the top angle and cut that angle on a mitre box. Repeat the angle cut for another dowel.

Next, determine where to put the porch posts; I suggest about 1 inch in from the side and about 1¼ inches back, but check to see how that suits your setup. Get the measurements accurate; then turn the birdhouse upside down and transfer those measurements to the base underside. Drill ¾-inch holes so the dowels can be inserted to touch the porch-roof line. Push the mitred dowels into the holes until they reach the roof and the angles match. Mark the dowel to cut it square with the porch.

Make the cut and reinsert the dowels in the holes. After the slanted edge passes through the base, coat it and the last ¾-inch of the dowels with glue. Push the dowels so they mate with the roof line and are flush with the underside of the base.

Once the house has been sitting long enough for the glue to set (setting takes about one hour, but wait two to be sure), sand it and place it where you wish. If you've used pine, instead of redwood or cedar, this is the time to lay on a coat or two of various enamel finishes.

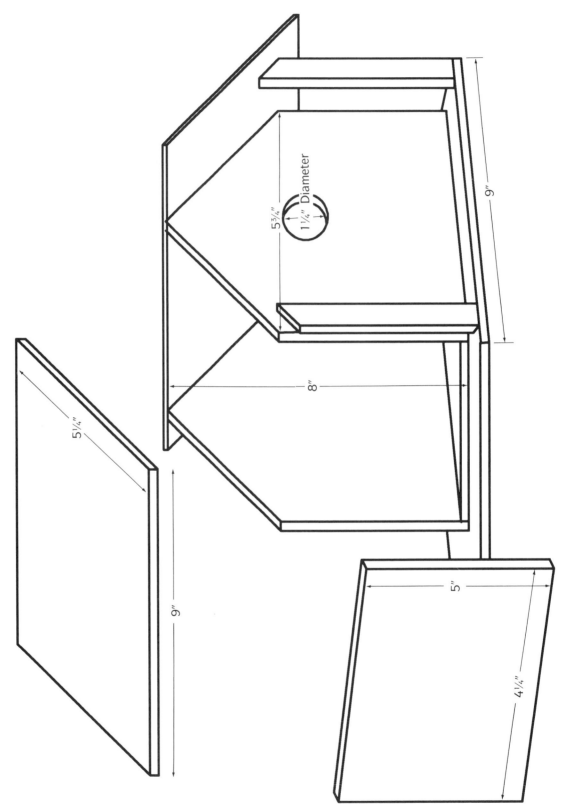

Illus. 7–87. Birdhouse with porch.

Birdhouse Plans

HACIENDA-STYLE BIRDHOUSE

Some birdhouses are little more than simple boxes, and this is one of them (Illus. 7–88). The addition of a few dowels as roof joists keeps things from getting *too* simple.

Materials

One piece of 1 × 9 × 9″ pine, for the *roof*
Two pieces of 1 × 5½ × 5½″ pine, for the *sides*
Two pieces of 1 × 6 × 7″ pine, for the *front and back*
One piece of 1 × 5½ × 7″ pine, for the *base*
Eight ⅜″ diameter × 11″ long dowels, for the *joists*
Two #8 × 1¼″ square-drive screws with super-round washer heads
Sand-colored paint
Brown paint
Weatherproof wood glue

Tools

Table saw
Handsaw
Mitre saw
Drill
1½″ Forstner drill bit or hole saw
⅛″ drill bit for pilot holes
Claw hammer (10 or 13 ounces)
Nail set
Measuring tape
Square
Pneumatic nailer
Finish sander
Sandpaper (100 grit)
Paintbrush

*   *   *

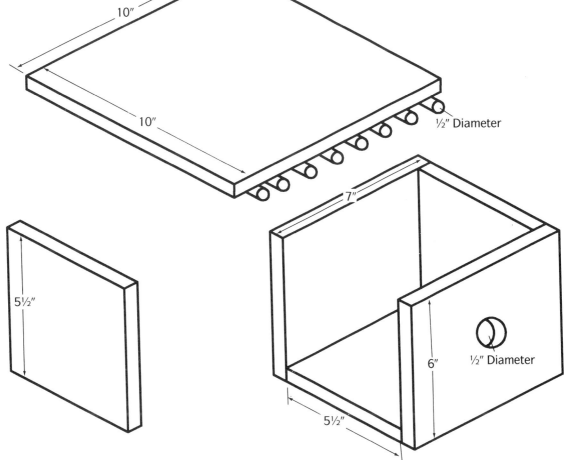

Illus. 7–88. Simple hacienda birdhouse.

Instructions

This birdhouse is easy to make. There are no mitres, bevels or curves to cut. Cut the pieces to the sizes indicated in the Materials list, and paint the outside ends of the dowels—about 1½ inch at each end—dark brown. Coat the underside of the roof with glue after marking the top for about equal spacing of the dowels. Place the dowels on the underside of the roof and gently lower the roof, trying not to disturb the dowel positions. Then drill the 1½-inch entry hole.

Start the basic box assembly by placing the base in a vise. Coat one edge of the base with glue and nail the back in place. Remove the unit from the vise and glue and nail the front to the other edge of the floor. Run glue lines on the sides and floor, and then insert and nail one side in place. Place the other side and also glue and nail it. Then spray the basic box with sand-colored paint.

By this time, the roof should be ready. Set it in place and run pilot holes for the screws that make the roof removable so the house can be cleaned out. Paint the roof, and you've got another adobe-style birdhouse.

HACIENDA BIRDHOUSE #2

This model (Illus. 7–89) is almost identical to the previous one. The only difference is the addition of a slant to the roof. This, and its dowel roof joists, livens up the birdhouse a little.

Material

One piece of 1 × 8½ × 10″ pine, for the *roof*
Two pieces of 1 × 5½ × 5½″ pine, for the *sides*
One piece of 1 × 1 × 6″ pine, for the *front*
One piece of 1 × 7 × 5″ pine, for the *back*
One piece of 1 × 5½ × 7″ pine, for the *bottom*
Eight ⅜″ diameter × 11″ long dowels, for the *joists*
Two #8 × 1¼″ square-drive screws with super-round
    washer heads
Sand-colored paint
Brown paint
Weatherproof wood glue

Illus. 7–89. Hacienda birdhouse #2.

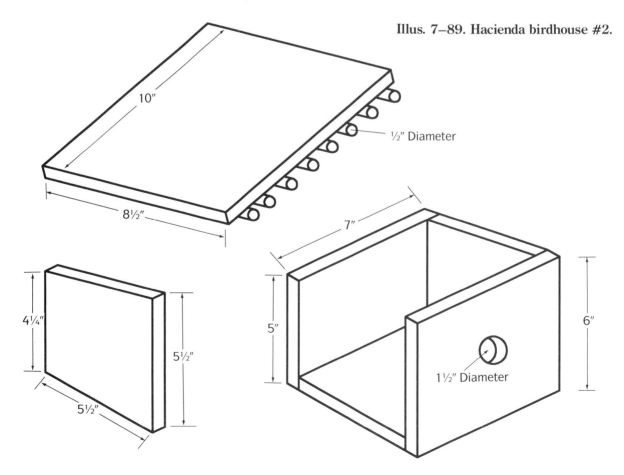

Table saw
Handsaw
Mitre saw
Drill
1½″ Forstner drill bit or hole saw
⅛″ drill bit for pilot holes
Claw hammer (10 or 13 ounces)
Nail set
Measuring tape
Square
Pneumatic nailer
Finish sander
Sandpaper (100 grit)
Paintbrush

Instructions

This hacienda-style birdhouse is almost as easy to make as the first one; the only difference is that two additional mitre cuts are made. Cut the pieces to their sizes indicated in the Materials List, and paint the outside ends—about 1½ inch at each end—of the dowels dark brown. Coat the underside of the roof with glue after marking the top for about equal spacing of the dowels. Place the dowels on the underside of the roof and gently lower the roof—try not to disturb the dowel positions.

Next, cut the mitres on the sides, making the cut starting 5½ inches up on the front and dropping to 4¼ inches on the back. Then drill the 1½-inch entry hole.

Start the basic box assembly by placing the base in a vise. Coat one edge with glue, and nail the front to the base. Remove the unit from the vise and glue and nail the back to the other edge of the base. Run glue lines on the sides, and nail it in place. Place the other side and glue and nail it in place in the same manner. Then paint the basic box a sand color.

When the roof is ready, set it in place and run pilot holes for the screws that make the roof removable so the house can be cleaned out. Paint the roof, and you've got another adobe-style birdhouse.

FLICKER HOUSE

A flicker house (Illus. 7–90) is also suitable for a screech owl if it has a 3-inch diameter entry hole instead of the 2½-inch one for this one, and can work for flycatchers if the hole is reduced to 2 inches in diameter. The red-headed woodpecker likes a slightly smaller floor and a 2-inch-diameter hole, but even with a 3-inch hole and an enlarged base, this birdhouse still might not be able to attract a pileated woodpecker.

Materials

One piece of ¾ × 12 × 20″ exterior-grade plywood, for the *front*
Two pieces of ¾ × 7 × 12¾″ exterior-grade plywood, for the *sides*
One piece of ¾ × 7½ × 11⅜″ exterior-grade plywood, for the *back*
One piece of ¾ × 8 × 7½″ exterior-grade plywood, for the *roof*
One piece of ¾ × 6¾ × 5¾″ exterior-grade plywood, for the *floor*
One piece of ½″ diameter × 4″ long dowel, for the *perch*
Two #8 × 1¼″ square-drive screws with super-round washer heads
#4 galvanized finishing nails
Wood filler
Enamel finishes in your choice of colors

Tools

Table saw
Handsaw
Band saw
Mitre saw
Drill
2½″ Forstner drill bit or hole saw
½″ drill bit for dowel perch, if desired
⅛″ drill bit for pilot holes
Claw hammer (10 or 13 ounces)
Nail set
Measuring tape
Square
Pneumatic nailer
Finish sander
Sandpaper (100 grit)
Paintbrush

Instructions

Cut all pieces to their rough sizes and then set up the front piece for cutting on the band saw. The bottom arc has an 8-inch radius, while the top arc has a 3-inch radius. Cut and sand these radii smooth. Drill the 2½-inch-diameter entry hole 14 inches up the front, and space the perch dowel hole at least 5 inches below that.

Cut the back to 11⅜ × 7½ inches, and mitre the sides

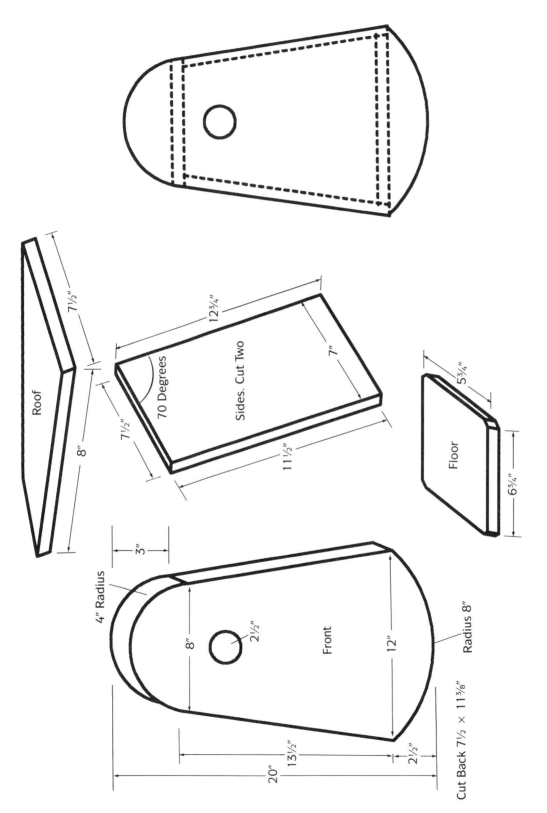

Illus. 7–90. Flicker house.

Roof

7½"

8"

12¾"

Sides. Cut Two

70 Degrees

7½"

7"

11½"

5¾"

Floor

6¾"

3"

4" Radius

8"

2½"

Front

12"

Radius 8"

13½"

2½"

20"

Cut Back 7½ × 11⅜"

from 12¾ inches high at their fronts to 11½ inches at their rears. Bevel the front of the roof at 10 degrees, the top edges of the sides at 5 degrees, and the outside edges of the bottom also at 5 degrees.

Start the assembly by gluing and nailing one side to the front, with the side and the top held so the bottom of the arc is where the bottom edge of the side touches. Remove the unit from the vise and nail and glue on the second side. Add the back, again using nail and glue to fasten it. The bottom, or floor, goes in next, again with nail and glue.

Carefully fit the top and drill the pilot holes for the #8 square-drive screws. When those are run in, the top can be quickly removed so you can clean out the flicker house.

Finally, fill all exposed plywood edges with wood filler, allow them to dry, and sand them smooth. Paint the birdhouse in your choice of colors.

EASY-TO-DECORATE BIRDHOUSE

This birdhouse (Illus. 7–91), meant for bluebirds, warblers, and tree swallows, has a true birdhouse style, with gabled ends, but can be easily painted in any style—and the use of different woods, such as cedar, redwood, or pieces of exotics, can add a touch that paints may not.

Materials

Two pieces of 1 × 8¼ × 5⅛″ pine or cedar, for the *roof*
Two pieces of 1 × 6 × 7⅞″ pine or cedar, for the *front and back*
Two pieces of ½ × 5⅛ × 6¼″ pine or cedar, for the *sides*
One piece of 1 × 6¼ × 5″ cedar, for the *floor*
One ⅜″ diameter × 3″ long dowel, for the *perch* (optional)
Clear finish (for cedar)
Enamel or paint finish (for pine)
Weatherproof wood glue
Two #8 × 1¼″ square-drive screws with super-round washer heads
#4 galvanized finishing nails

Tools

Table saw
Handsaw
Mitre saw
Drill
1½″ Forstner drill bit or hole saw
⅜″ drill bit, for dowel perch
⅛″ drill bit, for pilot holes
Claw hammer (10 or 13 ounces)
Nail set
Measuring tape
Square
Pneumatic nailer
Finish sander
Sandpaper (100 grit)
Paintbrush

Instructions

Cut the pieces to size and check them for square. This is another project that requires minimal tools, although, as almost always is the case, it's more easily and quickly built with a few power tools. Cut the 45-degree mitres for the front and back. Again, tape the two pieces together, being careful to align edges that will remain, to reduce cutting time and increase accuracy. Bevel one edge on each roof board at the same 45 degrees.

Begin the assembly with one side in the vise, aligning one side of the front carefully with the bottom of the side and keeping the edges flush. Check the fit of the side, spread glue on it, and nail it. Remove the assembly from the vise and attach the other side. Place the unit on its front and glue and nail the back in place. Next, assemble the two roof pieces on the gable ends, using glue and nails.

The bottom needs to be checked for fit, and is best made with ½ inch of each corner clipped off at a 45-degree angle. Place the bottom for a moderately loose fit, and drill pilot holes for screws that allow it to be easily removed. Run screws in; then back them out and remove the bottom. Then sand the house lightly, painting it colors to suit your taste.

This house installs easily. Just drive a screw down through the floor into the top of a post, and then reattach the rest of the birdhouse to the floor.

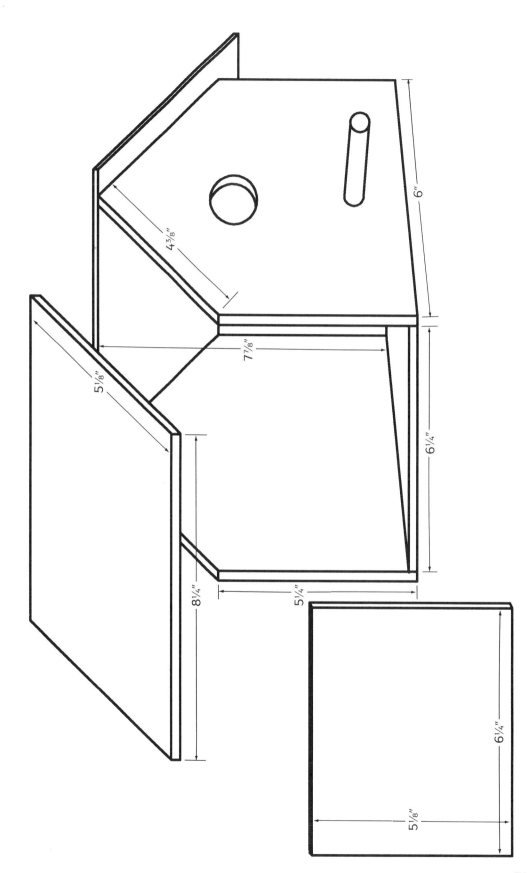

Illus. 7–91. Easy-to-decorate birdhouse.

APPLE-FRONT BIRDHOUSE

Fruit seems to make a popular decoration these days, and is something I enjoy, so here's a simple birdhouse for warblers, with the hopes the apple will at least keep the need for a doctor away (Illus. 7–92 and 7–93). The plan is suitable for warblers, but adding 1 inch to each side width, 2 inches to each side height, and, of course, the size of the roof, floor and apple make it suitable for bluebirds. (The pattern is easily increased on any copy machine that enlarges.)

Materials

One piece of 1 × 7½ × 9½″ pine, for the *apple* (The stem is optional, and if you decide not to use it, or to use it with other material, use a 7½ × 7½″ pine square for the apple.)

Two pieces of 1 × 5½ × 5″ pine, for the *front and back*

Two pieces of 1 × 5 × 4″ pine, for the *sides*

One piece of 1 × 6 × 6½″ pine, for the *roof*

One piece of 1 × 4 × 4″ pine, for the *floor*

⅜″ diameter × 3″ long dowel, for the *perch* (optional)

#4 galvanized finishing nails

Two #8 × 1¼″ square-drive screws with super-round washer heads

Weatherproof wood glue

Red water-based enamel paint

White water-based enamel paint

Wood filler

Tools

Table saw

Band saw with scrolling blade, or scroll saw

Handsaw

Mitre saw

Drill

1½″ Forstner drill bit or hole saw

⅜″ drill bit, for perch dowel hole (optional)

⅛″ drill bit, for pilot holes

Claw hammer (10 or 13 ounces)

Nail set

Measuring tape

Square

Pneumatic nailer

Finish sander

Sandpaper (100 grit)

Paintbrush

Instructions

Start by laying out and cutting all the square pieces, checking the cuts for square. Find the location of the entry hole on the piece of wood for the apple pattern, and mark its middle (at least 3 inches from the bottom of the birdhouse to the lower lip of the hole is needed). Also locate the hole for the dowel, which you may drill now if you wish. Do *not* drill the entry hole yet, as that needs to be drilled through both layers. Lay out the apple pattern on its workpiece and tape it down. (When I'm building these types of project, I print extras on my laser printer, but a copier can also be used; either way, you've always got an original to work with later. Use the first cutout as a pattern for the rest, if you're making more than one.) Cut the apple, and sand its edges carefully.

Next, paint the apple and allow it to dry. Then assemble the box by placing one side in the vise, lining up the front, and gluing and nailing it in place. Remove these pieces from the vise to attach the other side with glue and nails. Flip the assembly onto its front and attach the back, keeping the box square. Check the fit of the bottom, and insert it; it should fit fairly loosely. Drill pilot holes and temporarily assemble the bottom with square-drive screws, one in each side.

With the entry hole drilled, and the roof assembly just about ready, sand and paint the box your choice of color; I've listed white, mainly because I had white and blue paint on hand and felt blue would be too dark; but any color you choose works as well. Make sure to remove the floor before painting, unless you want the screws the same color as the basic birdhouse.

Place the apple on the front of the birdhouse box; use glue and nails here, and make sure to keep nails out of the area you'll be drilling for the entry hole.

Even with glue and nails, give the front a couple of hours to dry before drilling the entry hole. Do this not because the front needs the structural help of a glue set, but to keep wet glue from getting on your Forstner bit, which is not good for the tool, even though the amount transferred is minimal. Drill the hole and paint the inside edges.

Next, glue and nail the roof in place. Finally, check for any touchups needed on the paint, and find a location for your healthful home.

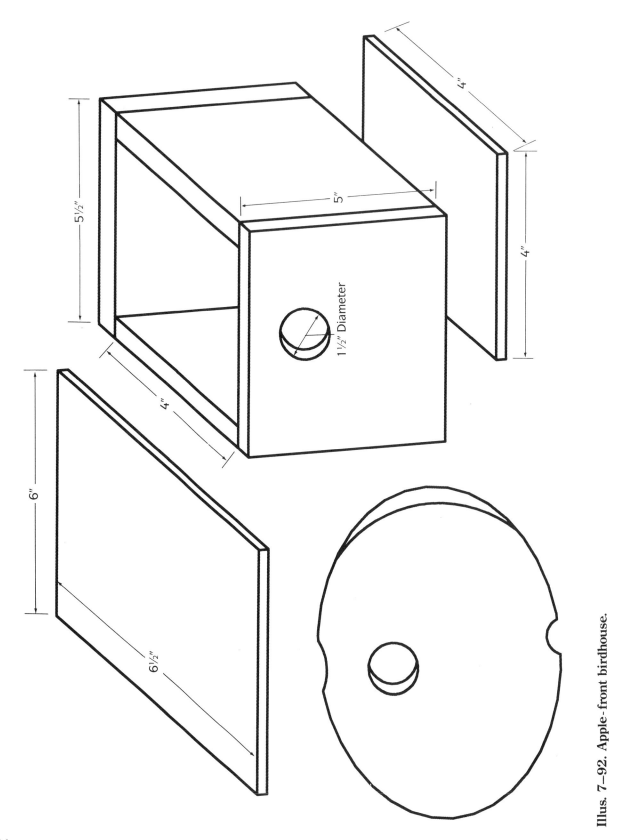

5½"

5"

4"

4"

4"

1½" Diameter

6"

6½"

Illus. 7–92. Apple-front birdhouse.

Birdhouse Plans

Illus. 7–93. This apple pattern is 75 percent of its original size.

GABLED CHICKADEE HOUSE

Chickadees remain among the friendliest of birds—that may be because they're so small the predators tend to ignore them—so that a yard full of these tiny ever-moving specks is also full of cheerful noise. This gabled chickadee house (Illus. 7–94) easily mounts atop a fence or other post, and takes a very short time to make from ½- to ¾-inch material.

Materials

One piece of 1 × 7¼ × 5″ pine, for the *roof part*
One piece of 1 × 6½ × 5″ pine, for the *roof part*
Two pieces of 1 × 6 × 9″ pine, for the *front and rear*
One piece of 1 × 4 × 4″ pine, for the *floor*
Two pieces of ½ × 4 × 7″ pine, for the *sides*
One ¼″ diameter × 3″ long dowel, for the *perch* (optional)

Weatherproof glue
#4 galvanized finishing nails
Two #8 × 1⅛″ square-drive screws with super-round washer heads
Enamel paints in a variety of colors, as you choose

Tools

Table saw
Band saw
Handsaw
Mitre saw
Drill
1⅛″ Forstner drill bit or hole saw
¼″ drill bit, for perch dowel hole (optional)
⅛″ drill bit, for pilot holes
Claw hammer (10 or 13 ounces)
Nail set

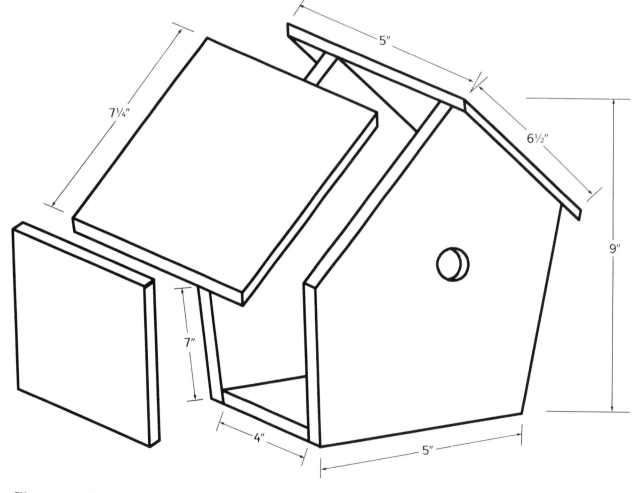

Illus. 7–94. Gabled chickadee house.

Measuring tape
Square
Pneumatic brad nailer
Finish sander
Sandpaper (100 grit)
Paintbrush (several, for different-colored paints)

Instructions

Make 50-degree mitre cuts on the front and back immediately after cutting all pieces to size. Not all mitre saws, power or otherwise, will open out this far, but my Ryobi 8½″ sliding compound and Makita saws do. In fact, the Makita saw will make 55-degree cuts, if needed. Bevel the roof halves about 20 degrees; they will overlap at their peaks during assembly.

Cut the lower tapers on the front and back simply by marking the ½-inch taper and using a handsaw or band saw to rip it off. Then drill the 1⅛- and ¼-inch holes in the front, placing the larger hole's middle at 6 inches up from the bottom of the front and centering the hole from side to side. The dowel perch is positioned about 2 to 3 inches from the bottom and is, of course, centered.

Next, begin assembly. Place one side in the vise and glue and nail the front to it, keeping both sides' outside flush and their bottoms even. Remove the assembly from the vise and repeat the process with the other side, after which you can glue and nail the back in place. Stand the unit upright and install the roof so that the overhang is at the front; place the shorter piece first, and then overlap it with the longer piece. Drill pilot holes for the #8 × 1¼-inch screws and set the unit aside.

Next, check the fit of the floor—as with all birdhouse floors, too tight a fit isn't a good idea. I made 45-degree cuts on all corners of my floor, for drainage. Then glue in the perch dowel. Now, sand the entire unit lightly, and paint it as you desire.

*   *   *

FLYCATCHER SALTBOX

This saltbox (Illus. 7–95) differs greatly in size from our earlier unit, and is intended for birds such as flycatchers and maybe even a redheaded woodpecker. I suggest here you work with a laundry pen to draw in doors and win-

dows, although you may prefer to nail on the dollhouse versions.

Materials

One piece of ¾ × 7¼ × 17¼″ pine or plywood, for the *front side of the roof*
One piece of ¾ × 13 × 17¼″ plywood, for the *back side of the roof*
Two pieces of 1 × 10¾ × 12½″ pine, for the *end walls*
One piece of 1 × 9¾ × 15¼″ pine, for the *front wall*
One piece of 1 × 5½ × 15¼″ pine, for the *back wall*
One piece of ¾ × 13 × 18¼″ pine, for the *floor*
   (Optional: for making the floor and base the removable parts, for cleaning out the birdhouse)
One piece of 3¼ × 3¼ × 4″ pine, for the *chimney*
Two #8 × 1¼″ square-drive screws with super-round washer heads
#4 galvanized finishing nails
Wood filler
Two 1½″ patches of wire screening
Fast-set epoxy, for securing the screening over the holes
Enamel paints of various colors. (Most New England saltbox designs are painted white. You can paint the base white and touch up the windows, doors, roof, and chimney in other colors, for a very attractive birdhouse.)

Tools

Table saw
Band saw with scrolling blade, or scroll saw
Handsaw
Mitre saw
Drill
2½″ Forstner drill bit or hole saw
1″ Forstner bit, for ventilation holes in gable ends
⅛″ drill bit, for pilot holes
Claw hammer (10 or 13 ounces)
Nail set
Measuring tape
Square
Pneumatic nailer
Finish sander
Sandpaper (100 grit)
Laundry marker
Masking tape
Paintbrushes

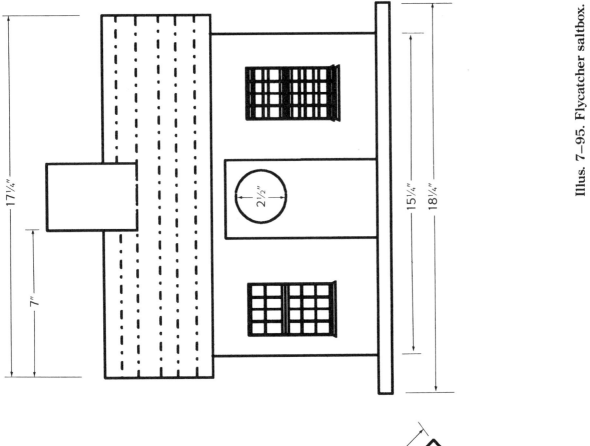

17¼"

7"

2½"

15¼"

18¼"

Illus. 7–95. Flycatcher saltbox.

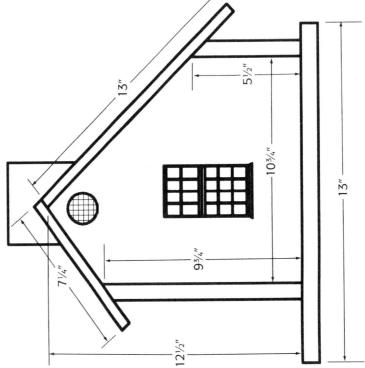

13"

5½"

10¾"

7¼"

9¾"

13"

12½"

Birdhouse Plans

Instructions

Begin by cutting all parts to the sizes indicated in the Materials List. If you desire a removable base section, cut the floor part. Cut the side wall's front mitre at 45 degrees, and either cut the second mitre at the same angle off of that mitre or mark out the decline from the 12½-inch to the 5½-inch point on the back wall. Bevel the top of the front wall at 45 degrees, and the top of the back wall to match the angle on the front wall.

Next, bevel the top end of the back roof section to match the ridge line of the front section; the front section, which is removable, will fit into the back section. You may have to experiment on some scrap stock to get this exactly right. Then mark and drill the entry hole and the gable-end ventilation holes. Using epoxy glue, glue the screening to the inside of the vent holes.

Start the assembly with one side in the vise, attaching the front with glue and nails. Remove the unit from the vise and attach the second side. The back goes on next, and then the base. If you wish to make the base removable, check the floor fit and attach the floor to the base with glue and nails. Drill pilot holes and run in the screws for a temporary fit right now.

Now, install the back part of the roof, using glue and nails. If the front part is to be removable, set it in place and drill pilot holes for the screws. If the base is to be removable, glue and nail the roof in place. Otherwise, screw it in place. Lightly sand all areas that need such work.

Set the chimney block against the gable end of the roof and mark the angle. Cut the angle on a band saw. Sand the chimney and paint it a bright red. At this time, you can paint the base grey or green, as you choose, and paint the basic house white. The roof may be any color you choose, but leave the part where the chimney attaches clear of paint. The chimney may be centered or placed nearer one end or the other, as you prefer.

With the entire unit assembled, and most of it painted, glue and nail the chimney in place. If the front roof section is made to be removable, attach the chimney only to that section. If the base is removable, glue and nail the chimney to both roof sections.

Touch up any paint that needs it, draw in a door and windows, reinstall the screws, and you're ready to find an area for your flycatcher saltbox.

MARTIN KEEP

A second simple martin house (Illus. 7–96) seems in order, since these useful birds are claimed to solidly cut into an area's insect population. This model of a Norman keep is made of ¾-inch-thick exterior plywood, with a removable roof for cleaning out the birdhouse. While the crenellations look difficult to build, they are easily cut with a hand or band saw, after which a good ¾-inch chisel will remove even plywood waste quickly.

Materials

One piece of ¾ × 24 × 16″ plywood, for the *front*
One piece of ¾ × 24 × 8¾″ plywood, for the *back*
Two pieces of ¾ × 22½ × 6¾″ plywood, for the *bottom and roof*
Two pieces of ¾ × 6 × 8″ plywood, for the *ends*
Three pieces of ½ × 6 × 7¼″ plywood, for the *dividers*
Weatherproof wood glue
#4 galvanized finishing nails
Wood filler
Masonry grey paint
Laundry marker with a moderately wide nib
Four #8 × 1¼″ square-drive screws with super-round washer heads

Tools

Table saw
Band saw or scroll saw
1″ wood chisel
Handsaw
Mitre saw
Drill
2½″ Forstner drill bit or hole saw
⅛″ drill bit, for pilot holes
Claw hammer (10 or 13 ounces)
Nail set
Measuring tape
Square
Pneumatic nailer
Finish sander (an oscillating spindle sander is nice, too, to sand down the filler in the holes)
Sandpaper (100 grit)
Paintbrush

Instructions

Cut all parts to their final sizes. Use either the band saw or a handsaw to cut the tower free on the front of the

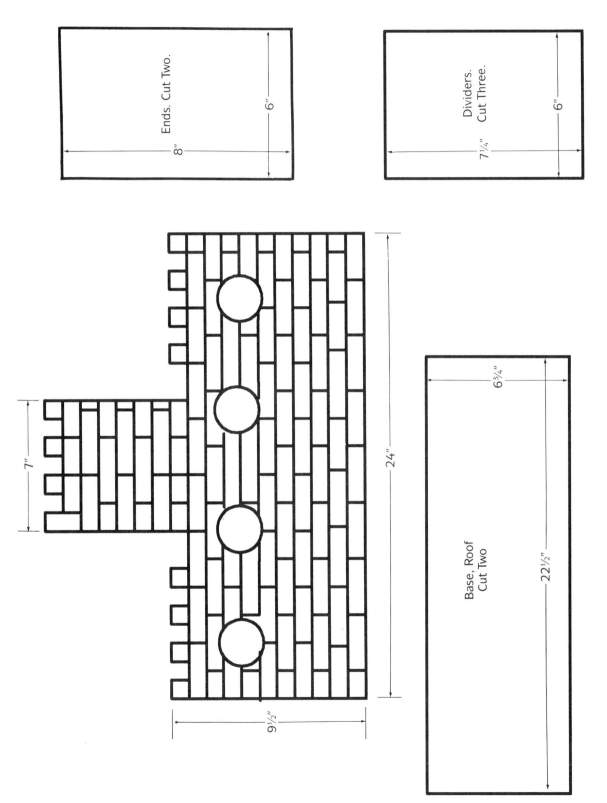

Ends. Cut Two.

8"

6"

Dividers. Cut Three.

7¼"

6"

Base, Roof Cut Two

6¾"

22½"

24"

9½"

7"

Illus. 7-96. Martin keep.

castle. Mark the crenellations at 1-inch intervals, and cut them with a handsaw or band saw to their proper depth. Use the 1-inch chisel to cut out waste material, and immediately fill the exposed edges with wood filler.

Once the wood filler has dried, paint the exterior of the front and mark the areas for the holes on the masonry paint with the laundry marker. Select your own intervals, but holes at intervals of 1 inch vertically and 2 inches horizontally seem to work well.

Next, mark out and drill the 2½-inch holes, allowing at least 5 inches beneath the lower edge of the holes (6¼ inches to the middle of the holes from the bottom of the workpiece). Sand the holes and fill their edges. Now, place the floor in a vise and run a good bead of glue along its edge. Align the front on the floor, making sure each end has ¾ inch left to accept the ends, and drive nails every 4 inches to produce a tight glue-nail joint. Next,

glue and nail the end walls to the front and the base.

The back goes on next. Once that's in place, sand the assembly lightly, except the already painted front. Then install the dividers, separating each of the four chambers so they're as close to equal in size as possible. I've specified ½-inch-thick material here so as to waste as little side-to-side space as possible. Glue and nail through the front and rear walls.

Now, check the fit of the roof, and install two #8 screws down into the back, and one into each end. Then check for nail holes that need filling, areas that need sanding, and any other problems. Sand lightly, if it is required, and coat the rest of the martin keep with grey paint. You may want to continue the stone patterns all around the birdhouse.

This martin house installs easily on any pole of suitable height.

APPENDICES

Birdhouse Dimensions

(All measurements in inches, unless otherwise stated)

Bird	Floor Size	Entry-Hole Size	Distance Entry Hole Is Above Floor	Interior Depth	Distance Birdhouse Is Set Above Ground (in Feet)
Bluebird (eastern and western)	5 × 5	1½	6	8	5–10
Chickadee (black-capped, Carolina, and chestnut-backed)	4 × 4	1⅛	6–8	8–10	6–15
Finch (house)	6 × 6	2	4	6	8–12
Flycatcher (great-crested, olivaceous, and western)	6 × 6	2	6–8	1–10	8–20
Nuthatch (white-breasted and red-breasted)	4 × 4	1¼	6–8	8–10	5–20
Nuthatch (brown-headed)	2 × 3	1	6–8	8–10	5–20
Owls (screech)	8 × 8	3	9–12	12–15	10–30
Phoebe (eastern and black)	6 × 6	open one side	Not Applicable	6	8–12
Sparrow (song)	6 × 6	open all sides	Not Applicable	6	1–3
Sparrow (house)	4 × 4	1½	6–8	8–10	4–12
Swallow (barn)	6 × 6	open one side	Not Applicable	6	8–12
Swallow (purple)	6 × 6	2½	1	6	15–20
Swallow (martin or tree)	5 × 5	1½	1–5	6	10–15
Thrushes (American or robin)	6 × 8	open one side	Not Applicable	8–10	6–15
Titmouse (plain, tufted and bridled)	4 × 4	1¼	6–8	8–10	6–15

Bird	Floor Size	Entry-Hole Size	Distance Entry Hole Is Above Floor	Interior Depth	Distance Birdhouse Is Set Above Ground (in Feet)
Warbler (prothonotary)	4 × 4	1½	5	8	4–7
Woodpecker (downy)	4 × 4	1¼	6–8	8–10	6–20
Woodpecker (flicker)	7 × 7	2½	14–16	16–18	6–20
Woodpecker (hairy)	6 × 6	1½	9–12	12–15	12–20
Woodpecker (pileated)	8 × 8	3–4	10–12	12–30	12–20
Woodpecker (red-bellied)	6 × 6	2½	10–12	12–14	12–20
Woodpecker (red-headed)	6 × 6	2	9–12	12–15	12–20
Wren (brown-throated)	4 × 4	1	1–6	6–8	6–10
Wren (Carolina)	4 × 4	1⅛	1–6	6–8	6–10
Wren (house)	4 × 4	1	1–6	6–8	6–10
Wren (winter)	4 × 4	1 × 2½	4–6	6–8	5–10

GENERAL BUILDING GUIDELINES

As indicated in the chart, very little wood is needed to build any birdhouse, even those large enough for woodpeckers and owls. For these larger birdhouses, plywood becomes exceptionally handy, but otherwise most birdhouses are readily built out of 1 × 6, 1 × 8, and 1 × 10 dimension lumber of whatever type you have on hand or can readily find locally. As you collect material, remember that building for birds is different than building for humans: birds are unconcerned as to whether you have used a fancy design for a birdhouse (too much shiny enamel may cause them to stay away, though), but humans do. Do make sure, however, that you precisely size the birdhouse holes, in order to help keep other birds out of the birdhouses.

The chart will help you adjust the size of the designs to allow for a specific bird. For example, no birdhouse designs for owls or woodpeckers are provided in this book, but the flycatcher house needs only minor conversion to suit either one, and several other patterns can be quickly adapted for the same purposes. Many birds require only a change of entry-hole size to allow use of a 4 × 4 or 5 × 5 or 6 × 6 floor. Narrow an entry hole from 1½ to 1 or 1⅛ inch in diameter and you have adapted what was originally a warbler house into a wren house. If chickadees are around, a pair may find a birdhouse with a 1⅛-inch entry hole appealing. Exactness is a human requirement: Birds don't measure a place before moving in. If they can enter the birdhouse and are comfortable (snug) in the enclosure, without feeling trapped, they will live there. Get the overall sizes and hanging height of the birdhouse close to accurate, place it in an area in which the species to be attracted is known to live, and wait. The birds will come.

* * *

METRIC EQUIVALENCY CHART
mm—millimetres   cm—centimetres
INCHES TO MILLIMETRES AND CENTIMETRES

inches	mm	cm	inches	cm	inches	cm
⅛	3	0.3	9	22.9	30	76.2
¼	6	0.6	10	25.4	31	78.7
⅜	10	1.0	11	27.9	32	81.3
½	13	1.3	12	30.5	33	83.8
⅝	16	1.6	13	33.0	34	86.4
¾	19	1.9	14	35.6	35	88.9
⅞	22	2.2	15	38.1	36	91.4
1	25	2.5	16	40.6	37	94.0
1¼	32	3.2	17	43.2	38	96.5
1½	38	3.8	18	45.7	39	99.1
1¾	44	4.4	19	48.3	40	101.6
2	51	5.1	20	50.8	41	104.1
2½	64	6.4	21	53.3	42	106.7
3	76	7.6	22	55.9	43	109.2
3½	89	8.9	23	58.4	44	111.8
4	102	10.2	24	61.0	45	114.3
4½	114	11.4	25	63.5	46	116.8
5	127	12.7	26	66.0	47	119.4
6	152	15.2	27	68.6	48	121.9
7	178	17.8	28	71.1	49	124.5
8	203	20.3	29	73.7	50	127.0

Index